Nonpartisan

This book is not about politics. It is about leadership. The fundamentals of leadership excellence are not bound by party lines or exclusive to one side or another. No matter your political preferences, you can learn from the leadership strengths of each of the United States Presidents.

Positive

Every person and every leader has their flaws. This book does not focus on mistakes and weaknesses, it focuses on leadership strengths. Even with their individual weaknesses, each United States President achieved the most prestigious, powerful and influential position in the world—no doubt we can learn and benefit from their strengths!

Relevant

Leadership excellence is an increasingly vital asset in our ever changing, ever demanding world. Leaders must proactively improve their leadership and never stop learning. Those who seek leadership excellence realize the critical necessity of learning from other successful leaders—so why not learn from the United States Presidents?

Take your life, leadership and success to the next level. Improve and strengthen your leadership—and the personal, professional, and organizational success of those you lead!

PRESIDENTIAL LEADERSHIP

Learning from
UNITED STATES PRESIDENTIAL LIBRARIES & MUSEUMS

Donated to the wonderful People in Breckenridge, Colorado! Enjoy. I love your beautiful town!

Dan Nielsen

8-04-15

DAN NIELSEN
WITH EMILY SIRKEL

Copyright © 2013 by Dan Nielsen

All photos copyright © 2013 by Dan Nielsen with the exception of the presidential portraits on pages 11, 33, 51, 71, 89, 111, 133, 153, 171, 191, 209, 231, 253, and 271. The presidential portraits used in this book fall within the public domain and were obtained via http://commons.wikimedia.org.

Published by
Dan Nielsen Company
www.dannielsen.com
contact@dannielsen.com

Printed in the United States of America.

All rights reserved. No part of this book may be reproduced or transmitted in any form or by any means, electronic or mechanical, including photocopying and recording, or by any information storage and retrieval system, without permission in writing from the publisher, except for brief quotations in critical reviews and articles.

Readers should be aware that internet websites offered as citations or as sources for further information may have changed or disappeared between the time this book was written and when it is read.

ISBN: 978-0-9898150-0-0

With great respect and gratitude, I honor my mother and father, Ethel Harrison Nielsen and Robert Nielsen. Throughout great times and difficult times, my parents believed in me, encouraged me, and mentored me by living a life of love, faith, integrity, humility, kindness, and generosity.

Frequently, during my youth and thereafter, people made unsolicited remarks such as, "Your dad is the kindest man I have ever met," or "Your mother is a bright and talented woman with strong character, commitment, faith, and integrity."

In a million different ways, but particularly because of the impact of my parents, I am a blessed man! Nothing would please me more than for this book to honor my parents. I am forever indebted and I miss them daily.

– Dan Nielsen

⌐◠⁀◠⌐

I dedicate this book to my mom, who taught me to love reading and writing, to my dad, who has always modeled strength, confidence, and integrity, and to my husband, who grinned and kissed me when I told him I wanted to be a writer. Thank you for always believing in me.

– Emily Sirkel

CALL TO ACTION

This book is intended to be more than an interesting and informative peek into the lives and leadership of the United States Presidents. I have designed this book to be a tool for you to use in your journey toward improving your leadership strengths and developing leadership excellence. My hope is that by studying the leadership strengths of these fourteen former presidents, you will be inspired to identify and select key leadership strengths that you desire to improve upon in your own life and leadership.

If you truly desire to apply these proven strengths and improve your leadership, I urge you to skip ahead and start by reading the full Call to Action found on page 285. There I provide specific tips, strategies and suggestions to help you create and immediately apply:

A SUCCESS SYSTEM THAT NEVER FAILS

I strongly believe that you will receive far greater value from this book if you begin with the end in mind. Go ahead, I give you permission to read this book "out of order." Flip ahead to page 285 and read the Call to Action, then dive into the rest of the book.

What are you waiting for?

Contents

Preface

How and Why I Came to Write This Book

Over the course of my life I have had the privilege of traveling to every corner of the United States and just about everywhere in between. My never-ending quest to see and experience new things has taken me on an extensive decades-long journey throughout America the Beautiful. I've hiked through national parks and toured priceless art museums, dined in extravagant restaurants and grabbed lunch from mom and pop cafés, camped along sandy beaches and parked my motorhome among snowy mountains, browsed in hole-in-the-wall stores and savored the amenities of luxury shops, enjoyed thousands of sunsets and experienced a million other priceless adventures.

Throughout my extensive travels across America, I have also remained committed to being a lifelong learner. I don't merely skim through museums or take a peek at national monuments and historic sites—I stop, settle in, and study for hours and often days, capturing thousands of memories with my camera as well as my mind.

Somewhere along the way I discovered a unique national treasure known as the United States Presidential Libraries and Museums, operated by the National Archives and Records Administration (NARA). Through historic artifacts and interactive exhibits, these fascinating, nonpartisan institutions offer a unique window into the dramatic events and seasoned leadership of each of the last thirteen U.S. Presidents, within the context of history. I've always enjoyed American history, and as someone who's been in the business of leadership for more than forty years, I have long admired many of America's leaders, including the U.S. Presidents. As I began to explore these presidential libraries and museums, I quickly discovered that each one is brimming with intriguing history and powerful leadership lessons—a perfect destination for anyone who appreciates American history and leadership excellence like I do.

My fascination with the presidential libraries and museums started in Austin, Texas, when I chose to tour the LBJ Library on the campus of the University of Texas. Soon I visited a second presidential library, and then a third, then a fourth, and pretty soon I had explored every one of the thirteen presidential libraries and museums that are operated by the NARA. I also discovered and explored the Abraham Lincoln Presidential Library and Museum, which is not a part of the NARA's system of presidential libraries, but is just as fascinating and valuable as the rest.

True to my character as an eager seeker of knowledge, I chose to not merely tour each library and museum, but instead I carefully studied and extensively photographed each of these remarkable institutions, choosing to spend several days and repeat visits at many of them. As a result, I have a cumulative collection of more than ten thousand photos and a million memories from these incredible libraries and museums. I share a handful of my photos in the pages of this book, and hundreds more—in full color—on my specially designed resource website, www.presidentialleadershipbook.com.

Over the years, as I continued to experience these invaluable storehouses of American history and to learn about the remarkable presidential legacies preserved within them, I began to formulate the idea for this book. My intentions in writing this book are two-fold:

> FIRST, I am obviously passionate about these unique institutions, and I want to help share this national treasure with others. Sadly, many people have no idea that the presidential libraries and museums exist, and even those who do know about them often have a very limited understanding or appreciation for their value. I would like to change that.
>
> SECOND, I am passionate about improving my leadership and helping others to do the same. I strongly believe and frequently state that, "leadership excel-

lence is the ultimate strategy for success." No matter who you are or what role or position you're in, you influence those around you. Leadership is all about influence. Every person is a leader, and every person can be a better and more effective leader. I believe that through careful study of influential leaders—both successful and unsuccessful—every person can improve their leadership skills.

Having attained the highest elected office in America, the United States Presidents have reached the summit of American leadership and achievement, and are considered by many to hold the most powerful office and position in the world. Within this book I will examine a selection of leadership strengths demonstrated by these extremely influential leaders. I firmly believe, with careful study and intentional application, that every person reading this book can apply these proven leadership strengths and improve their own leadership.

The idea to write this book finally became reality in late 2011 when I met a talented young lady by the name of Emily Sirkel. Not long after our first meeting, Emily became my writing partner, and with the help of her thoughtful collaboration, detailed research, and excellent writing skills, my book—which quickly became "our book"—began to take shape. The pages that follow are a direct result of our collaborative effort and hard work, and would not have happened without the talents and dogged perseverance of my coauthor; for her partnership I am eternally grateful.

– Dan Nielsen

How to Use this Book
Intended Purpose and Reader Resources

The purpose of this book is to highlight selected leadership strengths demonstrated by the presidents, and to serve as an inspiration and tool for you to use as you focus on and improve your own leadership strengths. My desire is that this book also shed light on the value and purpose of United States presidential libraries and museums—a true American treasure.

I urge you to make this book your own. Whether reading it on paper or on a digital device, be sure to highlight, underline, write notes, and leave bookmarks as you read and study the book. By marking it up, making notes, and highlighting and sharing key quotes throughout the book, you will be far more likely to follow up and use the book and your notes to apply these strengths, improve your leadership, and achieve greater success!

While I encourage you to read the book as a whole, it can also be read in sections, as each chapter is designed to stand on its own. Each of the first thirteen chapters is dedicated to one U.S. President, his leadership, and the presidential library and museum that preserves his legacy. The last chapter is a bonus chapter, dedicated to one of the most admired presidents of all time, Abraham Lincoln.

Each chapter begins with my personal account of my visit to that particular presidential library and museum and includes a small sampling of photos from my trip. These personal narratives are purposefully brief, designed to provide an alluring glimpse into these unique institutions without going into great detail. In reality, I spent numerous hours and often multiple days at each presidential library and museum, carefully studying and extensively photographing the fascinating buildings and exhibits. My hope is that by getting a sneak peek, through my perspective, you will be intrigued and inspired to personally visit each presidential library and museum yourself. If you have even a remote interest in American history, the presidency, and leadership, I promise you'll find them fascinating! Please note that due to ongoing updates and occasional major renovations, some disparities may occur between what I have described or photographed and what may now exist at each library and museum—all the more reason to see them yourself!

The second part of each chapter features a brief historical narrative of that particular president and highlights selected leadership strengths that I believe he demonstrated and that we all can learn from. As you read through each chapter, I urge you to take note of the leadership strengths that you would like to improve upon and apply in your own leadership. It is my desire that in addition to being interesting and informative, this book will prove to be a useful and inspiring study guide for developing more effective leadership.

In the back of the book you will find a Call to Action and simple but effective *Success System That Never Fails* designed to inspire and equip you to focus on and improve your own leadership strengths. Don't just read this book and put it back on your shelf. Use it! Learn from it! Don't forget, "leadership excellence is the ultimate strategy for success!"

In addition to the Call to Action I have provided a simple-to-use index in the back of the book to help you locate and study the specific leadership strengths highlighted throughout every chapter. I have also included a listing of the sources utilized in the writing of this book, and a list of suggested resources for further study of the presidential libraries and the U.S. Presidents. Among these resources is a specially designed website, www.presidentialleadershipbook.com, where you can find additional information about the presidents and the presidential libraries and museums, interesting facts, inspiring quotes, hundreds of full-color photos from my collection, and much more.

This book is a companion resource to my presentation, "Presidential Leadership: Learning from United States Presidential Libraries and Museums." As an experienced and versatile speaker and facilitator for groups of any size, I am available for keynote presentations, breakout sessions, retreats, or facilitated discussions with smaller teams or groups. For more information about my presentations and speaking availability, please refer to page 298 or visit my website at www.dannielsen.com.

INTRODUCTION
WHAT THIS BOOK IS AND WHAT IT ISN'T

Why one more book about the presidents?

I realize that an ever-increasing collection of material on the United States Presidents is already available, including very informative and comprehensive biographies of each. This book is neither intended to be an exhaustive study of the included presidents nor merely a brief summation of their lives. Instead, I have striven to highlight specific leadership strengths demonstrated by each president, while providing sufficient but succinct biographical context. I have also provided what I hope is a unique window into the invaluable institutions that preserve the legacies of the U.S. Presidents.

What exactly is a presidential library and museum?

The presidential libraries and museums serve to promote understanding of the presidency and each president's place in American history by preserving and providing access to historical materials, and by creating educational and inspiring exhibits and programs. Each library and museum includes an archive and research facility available to registered researchers, and an extensive collection of galleries and exhibits open to the public. The museums have a mixture of fascinating permanent galleries as well as special temporary exhibits that feature a variety of unique themes, artifacts and displays that change from year to year. Mindful of changing times and advancing technology, the libraries and museums continually make small updates to their facilities and exhibits, as well as occasional major renovations as needed.

Thirteen of the fourteen presidential libraries and museums featured in this book are nonpartisan federal institutions operated by the National Archives and Records Administration (NARA). The fourteenth, the Abraham Lincoln Presidential Library and Museum, is also a nonpartisan institution, but it is not a part of the NARA's system of United States Presidential Libraries and Museums. The Lincoln library and museum is operated by the Illinois Historic Preservation Agency. For more information about the presidential libraries and museums, please visit the websites listed in the Resources section of this book on page 300.

What presidents are included in this book?

This book specifically features the last thirteen U.S. Presidents—Herbert Hoover through George W. Bush—whose legacies are currently preserved by presidential libraries and museums. I have also included a bonus chapter on President Abraham Lincoln. The scope of this book is intentionally limited to the leadership of these fourteen presidents and to the presidential libraries and museums that so artfully preserve their legacies.

Why don't all presidents have presidential libraries and museums?

According to the NARA website, the presidential library system did not formally begin until 1939, when President Franklin D. Roosevelt established a special facility through private funding and donated it and his presidential papers to the federal government. Congress later legislated this process with the Presidential Libraries Act in 1955 (amended in 1986), and thus the presidential materials of every U.S. President since Franklin Roosevelt have become the property of the federal government after each president's administration ends. Following Roosevelt's example, each presidential library and museum is privately planned and funded, then formally turned over to the U.S. government for operation through the NARA.

Before the advent of the presidential library system, former presidents or their heirs dispersed of the presidential materials as they wished, and sadly many valuable historic materials have been lost or destroyed. Though Roosevelt was the first president to establish a presidential library and museum, his one living predecessor at the time, President Herbert Hoover, later followed his example and also established a presidential library and museum. While many pre-Hoover presidential materials are preserved by the Library of Congress or divided among various museums, historical societies, and private collections, no NARA-operated presidential libraries and museums prior to Hoover's administration exist.[1]

Is this book political?

No. This book is not about politics and is not intended to promote any particular president or political party nor intended to condone or condemn any actions of these presidents. To the best of my ability, I have striven to remain objective and nonpartisan in my study of these presidents and their leadership strengths. While the conclusions drawn regarding individual leadership strengths are non-scientific and primarily a product of opinion, any perceived partisan indications within this book are accidental and do not necessarily reflect personal views.

Why focus on leadership strengths instead of weaknesses?

Without a doubt, no leader is perfect, and every one of the presidents featured in this book made mistakes. It would take countless volumes to address everything that these leaders are perceived to have done wrong. This book is not intended to be an exposé of every mistake or controversial decision these presidents made, but rather is intended to be a specific study of carefully selected leadership strengths.

I acknowledge that much can be learned by studying leadership weaknesses and attempting to avoid mistakes. However, for the purposes of this book I have chosen to focus instead on positive leadership qualities and strengths. I firmly believe that focusing on and improving your strengths is much more effective in the long run than dwelling on and trying to fix your weaknesses. I believe that this approach adds the most value, because as you build upon your strengths you will accomplish far more, and your weaknesses will diminish or even disappear.

Why these leadership strengths?

There are innumerable characteristics or qualities considered to be positive leadership traits, and dozens or even hundreds of those traits can be identified in the life and leadership of each president. I have included only a sampling of leadership strengths, chosen through my research and personal discretion, to feature in this book. I realize that some overlap of leadership strengths between these leaders is inevitable, but I have attempted to include as much diversity as possible. In many cases, the separate strengths I have featured are quite similar, but through my word choices and definitions I have attempted to highlight the slight nuances of meaning and significance. I realize that individuals may interpret certain words differently than I have intended them, so for clarification and the benefit of the reader, I have included definitions that I feel best describe and explain each strength as it pertains to that president.

Is this book affiliated with or endorsed by the NARA or the United States Presidential Libraries and Museums?

No. While I do have permission to use the photos I've taken at the presidential libraries and museums, and the information I've gleaned from the many exhibits and displays, I have neither sought nor received official endorsement by the NARA or any of the individual institutions. Any connection between the NARA and this book or myself should not be perceived as an endorsement.

Do you have more works related to presidential leadership?

This is my first book on presidential leadership, but it is a companion resource to my inspiring presentation, "Presidential Leadership: Learning from United States Presidential Libraries & Museums." I am a versatile and engaging presenter with years of experience speaking to and facilitating for groups of any size. In addition to giving keynote presentations I also lead breakout sessions and facilitated discussions. If you are interested in learning more about my presentations or would like to check my availability, please visit my website, www.dannielsen.com. If you would like to purchase copies of this book for your leadership team, corporate group, or association, bulk rates or package deals may be available upon request.

For more information about the presidents or the presidential libraries and museums, please refer to the Resources page at the back of this book, or visit my specially designed resource website at www.presidentialleadershipbook.com.

1

HERBERT HOOVER
PRESIDENTIAL LIBRARY & MUSEUM
West Branch, Iowa

My initial impression of the Herbert Hoover Presidential Library and Museum was of simplicity. Having previously visited several of the other newer and larger presidential libraries and museums, I was surprised by the small, modest stone building just off of Highway 80 in West Branch, Iowa. But as I began to tour and study the museum and grounds, I came to realize how appropriate the simplicity is. Herbert Hoover was born in 1874 as the son of a blacksmith and a seamstress and was raised in the tradition of the Society of Friends (Quakers). Though he rose from his humble beginnings to become a multi-millionaire and the thirty-first president of the United States, Herbert Hoover remained a modest, unassuming man throughout his life.

The 187-acre Herbert Hoover National Historic Site is not only home to the library and museum, it also preserves Hoover's humble Quaker upbringing. In addition to the library and museum itself, there is a Friends meeting house, a schoolhouse, a blacksmith shop, and

Herbert Hoover's Birthplace Cottage

several historic homes, including the tiny "shotgun shanty" where Hoover was born. This historic village was the site of America's thirty-first president's birth and early childhood. Now, just a stone's throw away from the cottage where he was born, visitors learn about his life and presidency and pay their respects at Hoover's final resting place.

While the Herbert Hoover Presidential Library and Museum is small compared to some of the others, it is no less intriguing. As I wound my way through the exhibits, I was drawn into the story of America during the turn of the century. It was truly fascinating to see how the nation, culture and government have evolved over the years. I learned more than I had ever expected about this humble man who became president, including the interesting fact that in 1927, while he was the Secretary of Commerce, Hoover became the very first person to appear in a television broadcast! I was intrigued by the exhibit featuring the early television technology—such a revolutionary and remarkable invention that has now become an ordinary part of everyday life.

As I continued to explore the late 1800s, the Roaring Twenties, World War I, the Great Depression, and more, I really got a feel for what life was like during Hoover's lifetime and presidency. By the

FIRST TELEVISION BROADCAST 1927

Exhibit featuring Hoover's appearance in the first television broadcast

time I stepped back out into the Iowa sunshine, I had gained a new understanding of the life and times of Herbert Hoover, and a greater appreciation for the opportunities and challenges Americans faced during the first half of the twentieth century.

Just up the hill from the library and museum is the gravesite, the final resting place of Herbert and Lou Henry Hoover. As I approached the gravesite, I noticed that there are no ornate plaques, elaborate gardens, or even presidential seals. Just simple white marble slabs with names and dates, guarded by a lone American flag. Standing at Hoover's graveside, I turned and gazed across the sloping hill and through the trees to his birthplace cottage, and reflected on the life and legacy of the thirty-first U.S. President.

After a full and meaningful life, Herbert Hoover came full circle, laid to rest in 1964 within site of where he was born ninety years earlier. As I took in the beautiful view, I realized with appreciation that the elegant simplicity of Hoover's final resting place speaks to his life and character, honoring a man who lived a humble life of public service and generosity. As I walked back toward the parking lot, I knew this place and Hoover's story would be one I would remember and revisit often.

One-room schoolhouse in historic West Branch

Society of Friends (Quaker) Meeting House

Did You Know?

Due to the necessity of work, Herbert Hoover barely attended and never graduated from high school, but he went on to attend the brand new Stanford University and graduated with a degree in Geology.

**Exhibit depicting children affected by the famine,
which Hoover strove to alleviate**

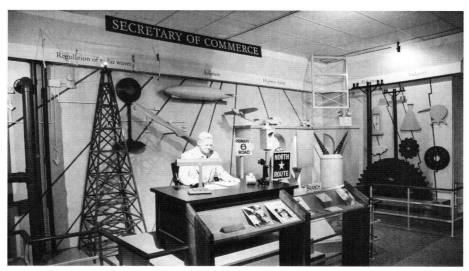

Exhibit depicting Herbert Hoover as the Secretary of Commerce

Did You Know?

*For private conversation, Mr. and Mrs. Hoover sometimes spoke
Mandarin to each other, which they learned as newlyweds living
in China.*

Exhibit featuring memorabilia, artifacts and photos from the 1920s

Display depicting the stock market crash of 1929

Did You Know?
On March 3, 1931 President Hoover signed the congressional resolution that officially made "The Star Spangled Banner" the United States' national anthem.

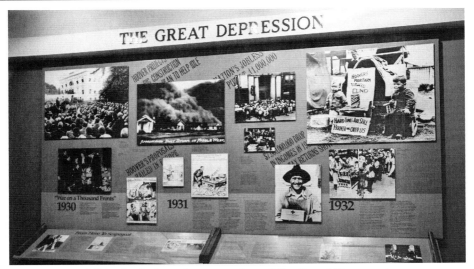

Exhibit depicting the struggles of the Great Depression

Gravesite of Herbert and Lou Henry Hoover

Did You Know?
Herbert Hoover was nominated for the Nobel Peace Prize five times.

View of Hoover's birthplace cottage from his gravesite

WHEN YOU VISIT...
DON'T MISS THESE:

- Hoover's Birthplace Cottage
- Historic School House
- Friends Meeting House
- Blacksmith Shop
- Gravesite of Herbert and Lou Henry Hoover
- The Roaring Twenties gallery
- First Television Broadcast exhibit
- The Great Depression gallery
- The Counselor to the Republic gallery

To see many more photos—in full color—please visit
www.presidentialleadershipbook.com/herbert-hoover/photos

"When there is a lack of honor in government, the morals of the whole people are poisoned."

"Words without actions are the assassins of idealism."

"Freedom is the open window through which pours the sunlight of the human spirit and human dignity."

HERBERT HOOVER
Determined, Responsive, Benevolent, and *Humble*

FULL NAME: Herbert Clark Hoover
LIFESPAN: 90 years (1874 – 1964)
TERM: 31st President (R) 1929 – 1933

Herbert Hoover rose from humble beginnings as the son of a blacksmith and a seamstress in West Branch, Iowa, to become a successful mining engineer, multi-millionaire, international humanitarian, and the thirty-first President of the United States. While the circumstances of the Great Depression made his presidency grim and short-lived, Hoover's leadership throughout his life made a lasting positive impact on millions of people around the world.

DETERMINED – Firmly resolved and unwavering in decision; driven, persistent, purposeful, focused.

Every leader will face adversity, deal with opposition, and make mistakes. Steadfast determination allows leaders to overcome great hurdles and achieve incredible accomplishments, making determination an essential characteristic of a strong leader.

Throughout his life, Hoover demonstrated profound determination and perseverance. Born into poverty and orphaned as a young boy, Hoover was determined to create a better life. In his own words, Hoover's boyhood ambition was "to be able to earn my own living, without the help of anybody, anywhere."[1] Raised a Quaker, he soon learned the value of hard work and integrity. Hoover grew to be an intelligent and earnest young man who though deprived of a full high school education, earned his way into the pioneer class of Leland Stanford Junior University, which opened in 1891.

Hoover graduated from Stanford with a degree in geology, but his first job out of college was anything but glamorous—shoveling ore in a California mine for two dollars per day. Hoover's determination and perseverance saw him through the backbreaking labor, and in 1897 he got the big break he needed—the London firm of Bewick, Moreing, & Co. was seeking a geologist. Included among the requirements for the position were that applicants be at least thirty-five years old and possess "a lifetime of experience." Determined that this was the opportunity he was looking for, twenty-three-year-old Hoover grew a beard, donned a top hat and tweed suit, and applied. He landed the job. This first chance at engineering led Hoover to the gold fields of the Australian outback and served to catapult his career as a mining engineer.

Over the next two decades Hoover built his fortune, traveled the world, and fulfilled his childhood dream of self-reliance and freedom from poverty. Hoover's life was successful, but marked by difficulty. Thanks to his unfailing determination and the close partnership with his beloved wife, Lou Henry, Hoover persevered through the trials of the Australian outback, the dangerous Chinese Boxer Rebellion, the horrors of two world wars, and the challenges of a presidency that coincided with the Great Depression.

⌐◦⌐

RESPONSIVE - Acknowledging and responding to need; responding readily and sympathetically to appeals or influences; acting in response to; understanding, sympathetic.

It is no secret that talk is cheap; some leaders have a knack for saying what people want to hear, but lack sincerity and follow-through. Truly responsive leaders back up their words with effective action. They recognize need and they quickly wield their influence and authority to meet that need.

Hoover was an incredibly responsive leader, who endeavored to improve the wellbeing of everyone he could. History tends to remember Hoover more for his failures than for his accomplishments, and his name has been indelibly linked to the tragedy of the Great Depression and his inability to save America from its effects. However, before becoming president, Herbert Hoover was an international hero, credited with saving more lives than anyone else who had ever lived.[2]

Hoover was a man of moral integrity and a man of action. He possessed a strong sense of duty to help right the wrongs of the world. When he saw a need, he took action to meet it; when he saw a wrong, he did his best to rectify it. Hoover didn't wait to see if someone else would take care of a need—he recognized need and took initiative to resolve it.

As a mining engineer, Hoover's financial success and position of influence gave him great opportunity to respond to the needs around him. He had a heart for public service, and together with his wife, Hoover offered assistance when and wherever he could. He was in London when World War I broke out in 1914, and was called upon by the U.S. government to organize the evacuation of Americans stranded in Europe. The war effectively propelled Hoover into public service, and soon he was seeking ways to relieve the food crisis Belgium faced following the German invasion. Pooling his wealth with that of several friends, Hoover established the Committee for the Relief of Belgium, which raised millions of dollars and organized an unprecedented relief effort to offer humanitarian aid to the desperate country.

After America's entry into World War I, President Wilson sought Hoover's expertise as a judicious and efficient administrator, and appointed him as the U.S. Food Administrator to coordinate production and conservation of America's food supplies. Hoover performed admirably in this new role, and went on to head the American Relief Administration, which delivered much needed aid to war-torn Europe following the war.

In 1921 Hoover was appointed as the U.S. Secretary of Commerce by President Harding. Soon after his appointment, Hoover came across a desperate plea for help published by Russian writer Maxim Gorky. A devastating famine, considered to be the worst natural disaster in Europe since the Black Plague, was ravaging Russia, and thousands of men, women and children were starving every day. Gorky pleaded for help from the West, and Hoover responded. He realized that something needed to be done, very quickly, to stem the tide of death and despair. His past experience as an engineer and as a humanitarian equipped him with the skills and knowledge necessary to move large numbers of men and supplies, and he quickly set the wheels in motion to offer life-saving aid to the Russian people.

BENEVOLENT – Desiring to help others, charitable, philanthropic. Expressing goodwill; generous, kind, compassionate, considerate.

Benevolent leaders desire to improve the lives of those they lead, and they generously offer whatever support and assistance possible. This display of benevolent, empathetic leadership helps team members and followers feel that they are understood as well as cared about, resulting in more effective relationships. A leader's compassion and generosity will produce trust, respect, loyalty and appreciativeness, and often has positive implications far outreaching the leader's position.

Hoover's entire life was marked by compassion for others. By the 1920s he had already experienced great professional success, but he also still understood hardship. His goal of making a better life for himself was accomplished, and Hoover yearned to use his blessings to make the lives of others better as well. World War I had presented the opportunity for him to use his talents and influence for public service, and now he was in a position to do something about the Russian famine as well. Hoover knew that if America did not take action, the consequences for millions of Russian men, women and children would be devastating.

Providing the needed aid to Russia was a logistical nightmare—with poor transportation, difficult terrain, extreme weather, and severe diseases all working against the efforts of relief workers—but Hoover and his team were up to the challenge. However, equally challenging for Hoover was rallying the rest of America to support a country considered to be an adversary of the United States. Some argued that by offering aid to Russia Hoover would be helping the dreaded Bolshevik radicals. Hoover adamantly retorted, "Twenty million people are starving. Whatever their politics, they shall be fed!"[3] Hoover successfully rallied the nation and led America in providing life-saving food that fed millions of desperate people.

Hoover's compassionate concern for others was evident in all areas of his life. In a letter to their children in 1932, Lou Henry Hoover wrote that she could give innumerable examples of her husband "personally giving to help individual cases beyond the limit of wisdom as far as his own resources were concerned."[4] When it came to public service, Hoover gave away his salary to worthy causes, becoming one of two U.S. Presidents to do so. And even with the weight of a difficult presidency on his shoulders, Hoover couldn't resist small acts of kindness toward individuals. One cold New Year's morning at the White House, two men showed up so early for the public reception, which traditionally took place in the afternoon, that

President Hoover couldn't bear to make them wait out in the cold. The president invited the surprised gentlemen to come inside, where he then proceeded to eat breakfast with them.

Hoover was certainly generous, but also astute; he always looked for long-term solutions to the problems he addressed. He also believed in rallying private support and voluntarism to address the nation's needs rather than encouraging dependence on the government. He subscribed to the philosophy: "Give a man a fish, you feed him for a day. Teach a man to fish, you feed him for a lifetime." Hoover's sense of responsibility for the welfare of others was balanced with the knowledge and belief that teaching, enabling and empowering people to overcome adversity and take charge of their own destiny was ultimately the best solution and the best aid he could offer as a leader.

HUMBLE - modest and unpretentious; not proud or arrogant; courteous, respectful, unassuming, reserved.

Confidence is attractive, but cockiness or arrogance never is. The most successful leaders possess sincere humility while still leading with confidence. Leaders who choose not to boast about their accomplishments or lord their position over their subordinates earn much deeper respect and loyalty in the long run.

Hoover didn't believe in playing political games. Even when running for president he denounced mudslinging campaign tactics within his party, and while he allowed his accomplishments to be publicized, Hoover was never comfortable with grandstanding to win public approval. He was a man of humility, serving others not for public recognition, but purely because he believed it was the right thing to do.

When Hoover became the thirty-first President of the United States in 1929, many believed he had reached the pinnacle of success. It had been a long journey from the little cottage in West Branch, Iowa where he was born five and a half decades earlier. Hoover approached this new chapter in his life with great enthusiasm and energy, believing that it was here that he could do the most good. Sadly, Hoover's presidency coincided with the infamous stock market crash of 1929 and the subsequent recession that became known as the Great Depression. Though he had previously been considered "The Master of Emergencies" and "The Great Humanitarian," Hoover was less effective as a politician, and was unable to cure the economy and the woes of the nation. He was soon tagged as the scapegoat of the Great Depression, and his former popularity quickly vanished, dooming his presidency to a grim single term.

While his disdain for the game of politics and his refusal to exploit his benevolence for political and public favor may have crippled Hoover's reputation, it reflected his moral compass. At heart, Hoover was always a humanitarian, not a politician; he wanted to address real, important issues and help improve the state of the nation—he did not want to play the frustrating game of politics. Hoover chose to serve in public office not because of an ego or any political aspirations, but because he felt that was where he could do the most good. Unfortunately, the good he did during the Great Depression was not enough to stem the tide of despair flooding the nation.

Unsurprisingly, Hoover lost reelection to the charming Franklin D. Roosevelt, and in 1933 the nation's former hero left the White House in defeat. But Hoover wasn't finished; he was down, but he wasn't out. Regaining his focus and devoting his post-presidency years again to international humanitarianism as well as service to the local community, Hoover's determination once again rose to the surface. He did not seek the public limelight or even focus on repairing his reputation. Instead, he humbly did whatever he could to help his nation and the world as an elder statesman. Hoover went on to partner with future presidents and helped to improve the welfare of millions in need, applying his talent and past experience to the challenges America faced during and after World War II.

Though he never fully regained the popularity and widespread admiration he had enjoyed before the Great Depression, by the time of his death in 1964 Herbert Hoover was again held in high esteem by many of his contemporaries. At his funeral, the Quaker theologian who gave the eulogy said of Hoover, "His story is a good one and a great one… It is essentially triumphant."[5] No matter personal opinion of the thirty-first U.S. President, a lesson should be taken from the determination, responsiveness, benevolence, and humility of Herbert Hoover. With these leadership qualities, he truly accomplished great things.

2

FRANKLIN D. ROOSEVELT
PRESIDENTIAL LIBRARY & MUSEUM
Hyde Park, New York

The state of New York is beautiful year-round, but I especially love the summertime. Bright sunshine, vibrant greens and colorful wildflowers decorate the countryside on the ninety-mile drive north from New York City to Hyde Park. I enjoy the scenic route up Highway 9, which runs along the Hudson River at first, veers away for awhile, then meets back up at Poughkeepsie, just ten minutes south of the Franklin D. Roosevelt Presidential Library and Museum. The library and museum is on the grounds of the Roosevelt estate, just a short walk from the Springwood mansion, FDR's beloved home on the eastern shore of the Hudson River. Now a national historic site, visitors can tour the home, grounds, and expansive gardens, pay their respects at the Roosevelts' gravesite, and explore the fascinating life and times of the thirty-second U.S. President and First Lady as preserved in the library and museum.

On my first visit to the FDR Library, as I turned off Highway 9

Franklin Roosevelt's lifelong home, Springwood Mansion

and drove up to the estate, I was awed by the great old trees, exquisite gardens, and well-manicured lawns. I stepped out of my motorhome and felt like I was stepping back in time, into the world of wealthy American aristocrats who enjoyed the finer luxuries of life here outside the hustle and bustle of New York City. Here is where the longest-serving U.S. President was born and raised and where he continued to call home throughout his life. Here also is where he is buried, along with his wife, Eleanor, and their famous Scottish Terrier called Fala, whose full name was "Murray the Outlaw of Falahill."

I chose to start my tour by stretching my legs with a stroll across the grounds. I soon came to the gravesite, set within a lovely rose garden filled with bright splashes of color. After pausing to quietly reflect in the memorial garden, I continued my walk, smelling the vibrant flowers, enjoying the summer breeze, and admiring the exteriors of the historic Springwood mansion and various outbuildings. Soon it was time to begin my guided tour through FDR's home, where I enjoyed a unique peek behind the scenes of the Roosevelt family's life. Thirty minutes later I was back in the bright July sunshine, and I made my way to the library and museum where I began my trip through the annals of American history and politics.

By the time I stepped back into my motorhome and drove out

Outbuildings on the Roosevelt estate

onto Highway 9, my head was spinning with the sights and sounds of America as it was in the early twentieth century. I had a new understanding of the economic and political landscape of FDR's presidency, and a greater appreciation for the challenges he faced. I knew much more about his remarkable First Lady and the enduring legacy she forged. I felt deeper sympathy for the millions of Americans who endured the hardships of the Great Depression, and who mourned the death of the man who led them through it. I came away awed and inspired by what I'd seen and experienced.

My next visit to the Franklin D. Roosevelt Presidential Library and Museum was almost two years later, immediately after major renovations were completed and the library and museum were rededicated and reopened on June 30, 2013. Now, extensively updated with interactive multimedia exhibits and video presentations, the Roosevelts' story, set against the backdrop of American history, is told better than ever. While the renovations and facility updates are significant, I was very pleased to see that the historic appearance of the nation's oldest presidential library was preserved. Here within the small but remarkable building that was originally built and dedicated under the direction of FDR himself, endures the Roosevelts' incredible legacy and unforgettable story for all to see and experience.

Bronze sculpture of Eleanor and Franklin Roosevelt

First exhibit within the museum, featuring photos & videos from FDR's life

Did You Know?

Franklin and Eleanor Roosevelt were married on St. Patrick's Day in 1905, and President Theodore Roosevelt (Eleanor's uncle) gave the bride away.

Exhibit depicting desperate times during the Great Depression

Gallery featuring Roosevelt's first campaign and election

Did You Know?

Franklin D. Roosevelt was a fifth cousin of President Theodore Roosevelt, a fifth cousin once removed of his own wife, Eleanor Roosevelt, and a seventh cousin once removed of Winston Churchill.

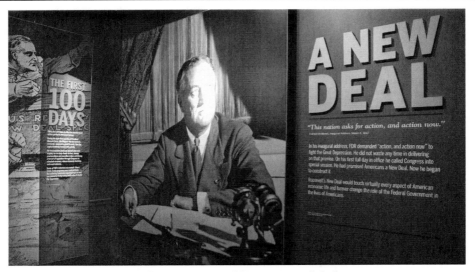

**Exhibit depicting Franklin Roosevelt's famous
"New Deal for the American People"**

Timeline and details of World War II

Did You Know?

Franklin D. Roosevelt was the first president to fly in an aircraft while in office.

Display featuring American war posters from World War II

Exhibit where visitors can listen to excerpts from FDR's "fireside chats"

Did You Know?
In June of 1939 President Franklin D. Roosevelt hosted a hot dog picnic for King George VI and Queen Elizabeth of Great Britain.

Actual office that FDR used at his presidential library and museum

**Display showing Eleanor Roosevelt's many pursuits
after her husband's death**

Did You Know?

President Roosevelt is the only president to have used his presidential library and museum while still in office.

Exhibit depicting Eleanor Roosevelt's relentless advocacy of human rights

Exhibit featuring the nation's reaction to
President Roosevelt's death and funeral

Did You Know?

Stamp collecting was one of Franklin Roosevelt's lifelong hobbies. By the time of his death his collection included over 1,200,000 stamps.

The gravesite of Franklin and Eleanor Roosevelt

WHEN YOU VISIT...
DON'T MISS THESE:

- Tour of Springwood Mansion (FDR's home)
- Beautiful grounds and outbuildings
- The Rose Garden and gravesite
- Freedom Court behind the museum
- The Roosevelt busts at museum entrance designed for the seeing impaired to touch and feel
- The actual office FDR used at the library and museum
- Exhibits depicting FDR's life after his illness, including the leg braces he wore and rare photos of him in a wheelchair
- Exhibits featuring FDR's four campaigns and elections
- World War II exhibits and the replica Map Room
- FDR's specially customized car, a 1936 Ford Phaeton
- Exhibits depicting FDR's death and funeral and America's reaction
- Eleanor Roosevelt gallery
- Additional artifacts in the museum basement, including FDR's oval office desk and model ship collection

To see many more photos—in full color—please visit
www.presidentialleadershipbook.com/franklin-roosevelt/photos

"Confidence... thrives on honesty, on honor, on the sacredness of obligations, on faithful protection and on unselfish performance. Without them it cannot live."

"The only limit to our realization of tomorrow will be our doubts of today."

"One thing is sure. We have to do something. We have to do the best we know how at the moment... If it doesn't turn out right, we can modify it as we go along."

FRANKLIN ROOSEVELT
Optimistic, Confident, Energetic, and *a Man of Fortitude*

FULL NAME: Franklin Delano Roosevelt
LIFESPAN: 63 years (1882 – 1945)
TERM: 32nd President (D) 1933 – 1945

Franklin D. Roosevelt, nicknamed "FDR," overcame incredible odds to become the thirty-second President of the United States. The only U.S. President to ever be elected to four consecutive terms, Roosevelt left an indelible mark on history; in a time of severe economic upheaval and looming war, he offered the American people something they desperately needed—hope.

OPTIMISTIC - taking a favorable view of events or conditions; hopeful, expectant, confident; positive, upbeat, cheerful, undiscouraged.

Optimistic leaders approach situations with a mindset of success. They recognize opportunity where others may see only uncertainty or despair. While the pessimist focuses on negative possibilities and sees challenges as excuses not to try a new venture or path, the optimistic leader sees and focuses on the positive possibilities and is willing to take appropriate risk for potential positive change.

Roosevelt's optimistic and jovial personality was one of the greatest contributors to his incredible success as a public figure. He was friendly and outgoing, and he genuinely enjoyed being with people. Roosevelt naturally exuded optimism and believed in the potential for a positive outcome, no matter how bleak the circumstances.

Roosevelt was a privileged youth who, as an only child, was doted on by his mother, Sara. Born and raised in Hyde Park, New York, young Franklin was raised to be a gentleman, receiving private tutoring at home until the age of fourteen when he was sent to attend Groton, a prestigious prep school in Massachusetts. At Groton, Roosevelt learned to overcome his shyness and make friends, something he had not had much opportunity to do before, due to his private tutoring. Soon Roosevelt's cheery personality overcame his initial timidity, and he became popular, developing close friendships. This upbeat attitude and ability to connect with others remained one of Roosevelt's signature attributes for the rest of his life.

After Groton, Roosevelt attended Harvard and Columbia Law School, followed by a few years practicing law in New York. In 1910, at the age of twenty-eight, Roosevelt launched his political career by running for a state senate seat. His youth, inexperience, and status as a Democrat in a largely Republican county all contributed to the odds against him in the campaign, but Roosevelt wasn't deterred, and his energetic and optimistic campaign paid off, winning him the seat.

The young politician's future looked very bright; he easily won reelection to a second term in the New York state senate, then soon after accepted appointment by President Woodrow Wilson to the position of Assistant Secretary of the Navy, where he distinguished himself as an energetic and efficient administrator. Roosevelt experienced some disappointments when he unsuccessfully campaigned for the U.S. Senate in 1914 and then again for the vice presidency in 1920 on a ticket with presidential nominee James Cox. Even so, he was still young and his political future looked very promising. After losing the 1920 election, Roosevelt returned to private life for what he believed would be a brief respite while he prepared for his next run for public office. However, the following summer his life took an unexpected turn.

In 1921, at the age of thirty-nine, Roosevelt contracted a debilitating disease diagnosed as polio. The ravaging effects of the illness caused him to lose the full use of his legs, which he never regained. Despite his significant physical disability and the extreme challenges it posed to his life and his political career, Roosevelt remained characteristically cheerful and optimistic. He did not consider the unfortunate turn of events to signify the end of his career. Slowed but not stopped, Roosevelt was unwaveringly optimistic, and against all odds, he continued to be active in politics while recovering from his illness. In 1928, his cheerful perseverance was rewarded when he was elected governor of New York, a position he held until attaining the presidency.

~◦✦◦~

CONFIDENT – sure of oneself, self-confident; having strong belief or full assurance; secure, sure; assertive, decisive, determined.

A healthy foundation of confidence allows a leader to be decisive and make difficult decisions. Leaders who demonstrate confidence engender trust in their followers and inspire greater loyalty—a critical asset, especially when the going gets tough. Only with confidence can leaders rally their people together toward a common cause in the midst of adversity or uncertainty.

Roosevelt's confidence in himself and in his ability to still contribute to the good of the nation despite his physical limitations led him to accomplish remarkable things. His self-confidence and determination not only led him to overcome the disadvantages of living with a disability, but to persevere as a strong leader in a time when despair threatened to encompass the nation.

Roosevelt's optimism and confidence played a key role in winning the presidential election of 1932. By the time of the election, the Great Depression had been ravaging the country for three years, and the American people were desperate for a glimmer of hope. Roosevelt offered just such a glimmer, promising effective action to turn around the economy and to help alleviate the symptoms of a suffering nation. An excellent communicator, Roosevelt confidently conveyed a vision for the future that sparked what little hope remained in the hearts of the people.

Weary from the extreme hardships of the recession, the American people chose to place their faith in the warm and optimistic Democratic candidate rather than in his opponent, incumbent Herbert Hoover. Roosevelt won the presidency in a landslide. Upon being sworn into office on March 4, 1933, he immediately took strides to enact a sweeping domestic agenda to turn the tide of the Great Depression. With great confidence and resolve, Roosevelt brought hope and healing to a discouraged nation.

The confidence of America's thirty-second president helped carry the nation through the Great Depression, and then through the Second World War. The bombing of Pearl Harbor on December 7, 1941 was a huge blow to the nation, resulting in over twenty-four hundred American casualties and more than one thousand wounded. In Roosevelt's famous presidential address to Congress the following day, he quickly and effectively rallied the nation behind him in war. While the country was still reeling from the devastating attack, Roosevelt boldly declared, "With confidence in our armed forces, with the unbounding determination of our people, we will gain the inevitable triumph, so help us God!"[1] This rallying cry received resounding applause, and within an hour of the speech Congress had passed a formal declaration of war against Japan, officially bringing the U.S. into World War II. In full expectation of victory, America's Commander in Chief confidently led the nation into war.

~᠆ᡋ᠊᠍᠋᠍ᢆᢀ᠊᠊᠍~

ENERGETIC – vigorous and full of life; desiring action; animated, dynamic, spirited, vivacious.

Contentment can too easily turn into stagnation. Leaders who never strive to push the limits and improve the status quo will never lead anyone to success. Leaders with energy are not content with the status quo; they yearn for action and desire results. Energetic leaders are compelled to action and eager to improve themselves and those whom they lead.

Despite his illness and resulting disability, President Roosevelt possessed a zest for life that often outshone able-bodied men many years his junior. Roosevelt's obvious energy dispelled the concerns of many Americans who had heard rumors about the extent of his disability. His robust, energetic personality helped to conceal his physical limitations, and the general public was vastly unaware that their president depended heavily on a wheelchair and the help of his aides for mobility.

As a politician, Roosevelt's boundless energy carried him through exhausting campaigns and difficult legislative battles. He always seemed to have the energy to keep going and persevere when faced with any challenge, and his contagious energy compelled others to follow his lead. Even when his health was failing toward the end of his life, Roosevelt sustained a vibrant energy that helped buoy the spirits of those around him.

When Roosevelt was sworn into office for his first term as president, he faced a nation in despair. In his inaugural speech on March 4, 1933, he said, "This nation asks for action, and action now."[2] Roosevelt was a man of energy and a man of action. In contrast to his more conservative and cautious predecessor, Roosevelt was eager to experiment and willing to take risks. He immediately threw his energies into creating his promised "New Deal for the American people"[3] by enacting a series of domestic programs designed to repair the country's worsening economic condition.

Though he hadn't laid out a clear-cut plan for his New Deal agenda, Roosevelt's energy and eagerness propelled his administration into action. Roosevelt firmly believed, "It is common sense to take a method and try it. If it fails, admit it frankly and try another. But above all, try something!"[4] In his historic first one hundred days in office, Roosevelt pushed fifteen major bills through Congress—an unprecedented achievement made possible because of his energetic and relentless efforts.

~◌◌~

MAN OF FORTITUDE – mentally and emotionally strong in facing difficulty or adversity; bold, brave, determined, resolute.

Courage has long been regarded as an essential quality of great leadership. The fear of failure, humiliation, pain, or discomfort has too often kept a leader from acting. Leaders who take action, determining that the potential results are more significant than their fears, are those who really succeed. When faced with daunting obstacles or fierce opposition, leaders with fortitude press on with determination, despite the risk.

Roosevelt demonstrated great focus, determination and bravery in the face of impossible circumstances. To this day, the public perception of those suffering from physical handicaps is plagued with stereotypes, and the capability of the disabled is often doubted. Roosevelt's determination to not only overcome his disability, but to continue to pursue roles in leadership and public office, was a demonstration of extraordinary courage and personal strength. He proved himself to be resilient and strong despite the debilitating disease that had robbed him of independent mobility. Years after her husband contracted the disease, Eleanor Roosevelt said of that time, "I know that he had real fear when he was first taken ill, but he learned to surmount it. After that I never heard him say he was afraid of anything."[5]

Illness and disability were certainly not the only hardships Roosevelt encountered; he served in public office during some of America's most trying times. The Great Depression hit the nation during Roosevelt's first term as governor of New York. Despite the extreme challenges every leader was struggling to overcome during this desperate period in history, Roosevelt was not disheartened and did not retreat in the face of adversity. On the contrary, he had the courage to take on a weight of responsibility far greater than the New York governorship—he chose to run for president. Having experienced firsthand the difficulties of leading a state during the recession, Roosevelt had a good grasp on the enormity of the task at hand for the person elected to lead the nation, and yet he was not deterred.

As Mark Twain is attributed with once saying, "Courage is not the absence of fear, it is acting in spite of it." Roosevelt faced the distress of the nation with fortitude and optimism, rising to the challenge. As president, he led America through one of its bleakest times of crisis, enacting a sweeping domestic agenda to combat the ills of the Great Depression and bring about the beginnings of economic recovery. Roosevelt faced opposition and hardships, but he persevered regardless of difficulty. When the Second World War threatened the safety of Americans, Roosevelt again faced adversity with great courage, resolutely leading his beloved country into war against the threatening nations. It was because of his optimism, confidence, energy and fortitude that Franklin D. Roosevelt was able to accomplish so much, leading the nation through crisis and toward the bright hope of its future.

3

HARRY S. TRUMAN
PRESIDENTIAL LIBRARY & MUSEUM
Independence, Missouri

As I drove up to the Harry S. Truman Presidential Library and Museum in Independence, Missouri, I was impressed by the stately one-story building overlooking a circular drive, long sloping lawn, and gently swaying oak trees. I couldn't help but think that the building looked very "presidential"—a fitting tribute to the man whose legacy is preserved there.

The very first exhibit that drew my attention when I walked inside the museum was a display featuring a handful of the more than 1,300 letters Harry Truman wrote to his beloved Bess during their sixty-two-year courtship and marriage. Harry and Bess met as children in Sunday school, and Harry immediately fell for the curly-haired, blue-eyed darling. They began dating as young adults, and after a long courtship, they were married in 1919. Their marriage, which lasted until Harry's death in 1972, was beautiful and intimate, as reflected in the hundreds of letters they exchanged over the years.

The famous sign that sat on Truman's desk during his presidency

Moved by their unique love story, I paused to read excerpts from several of the couple's letters before moving on to see the rest of the museum. The next thing that caught my attention was the famous sign that sat atop Truman's desk during his presidency: "The Buck Stops Here!" Displayed prominently in a glass case near the museum's entrance, the sign is a vivid reminder of Truman's commitment to integrity and personal responsibility.

As I wandered deeper into the historic building designed to preserve the legacy of the thirty-third U.S. President, I was reminded of and impressed by the number of significant world events that occurred during his lifetime. Harry Truman served his country during the First World War and presided over his country during the Second World War. As president, he made the momentous decision to engage in nuclear warfare to bring a decisive end to the war with Japan, and he saw the advent of the nuclear arms race known as the Cold War. Truman oversaw the Marshall Plan, which brought much-needed aid to war-torn Europe, approved the famous Berlin airlift, and joined eleven other nations in the forming of the North Atlantic Treaty Organization (NATO). On the domestic front, Truman integrated the United States armed forces and passionately pursued racial equality. He also pioneered the very first "whistle-stop" campaign,

Display featuring Truman's legendary "Whistle-Stop Campaign" of 1948

energetically traversing the country by train in the 1948 presidential race that resulted in a legendary upset. Defying the predictions of pollsters and pundits, Truman defeated his opponent, Thomas E. Dewey, on Election Day and went on to serve four more years as president in his own right.

I experienced each of these stories and more during my trip through history. I especially enjoyed the exhibit called "America in 1952," which features a large curved wall covered with dozens of *LIFE* magazine covers and layouts from that year, along with two TV monitors running commercials from that time period. What a flood of memories and nostalgia that brought back! By the time I emerged into the spacious courtyard of the museum and library, I was ready to stop and reflect for awhile. I paid my respects at the former President and First Lady's gravesite, admired the brightly burning Eternal Flame of Freedom, then enjoyed some quiet reflection in the beautiful, peaceful outdoor setting. The life journey of Harry and Bess Truman—from Independence, Missouri to Washington, DC and back—was truly remarkable. Together they left an enduring legacy, one that will be preserved, remembered, and appreciated by countless generations of Americans to come.

Replica of Truman's Oval Office

**Exhibit depicting the conflict between
President Truman and General MacArthur**

Did You Know?
Young Harry Truman met Bess Wallace when he was six years old, but they didn't begin courting until twenty years later, and they didn't marry until Truman was thirty-five.

Exhibit depicting the "boom" of the late 1940s enjoyed by many Americans

The actual office Truman used at his presidential library and museum

Did You Know?

*Harry S. Truman's middle initial, "S," does not stand for a name. It is a compromise between his two grandfathers' names: Anderson **Shipp** Truman and **Solomon** Young.*

Peaceful outdoor courtyard at the museum

Eternal Flame of Freedom honoring Truman's service during World War I

Did You Know?

Truman is the only U.S. President since the nineteenth century who did not graduate from college.

Replica of the original U.S. Liberty Bell

Harry and Bess Truman's home in Independence, MO

Did You Know?

A very determined Harry Truman memorized the eye chart so he could pass the eye exam and serve in the National Guard.

Gravesite of Harry and Bess Truman set within the museum courtyard

WHEN YOU VISIT...
DON'T MISS THESE:

- Truman's famous sign, "The Buck Stops Here"
- Exhibits featuring Truman's decision to drop the atomic bomb
- Gallery depicting challenges in postwar America
- The Cold War exhibits
- Whistle Stop Campaign and "Upset of the Century" exhibits
- America in 1952: *LIFE* magazine exhibit
- The Oval Office replica
- Legacy Gallery and Eternal Flame of Freedom
- Truman's personal office at the library
- Gravesite of Harry and Bess Truman
- Harry and Bess Truman home (offsite about 3/4 mile)

To see many more photos—in full color—please visit
www.presidentialleadershipbook.com/harry-truman/photos

"A pessimist is one who makes difficulties of his opportunities and an optimist is one who makes opportunities of his difficulties."

"In reading the lives of great men, I found that the first victory they won was over themselves... self-discipline with all of them came first."

"In periods where there is no leadership, society stands still. Progress occurs when courageous, skillful leaders seize the opportunity to change things for the better."

HARRY TRUMAN
Dutiful, Undaunted, Effective, and *Virtuous*

FULL NAME: Harry S. Truman
LIFESPAN: 88 years (1884 – 1972)
TERM: 33rd President (D) 1945 – 1953

Unlike many of his predecessors, Harry Truman did not strive to attain the presidency. Upon learning he was about to become president, Truman's immediate response was shock, not elation. Yet his performance as president has earned him widespread admiration from presidential historians, and his name is consistently listed among the best presidents in U.S. history.

DUTIFUL – performing without hesitation the duties expected or required of one. Devoted, faithful, committed, honorable; responsible, accountable, reliable, dependable.

Actions really do speak louder than words. Some leaders, and politicians in particular, have a reputation for speaking empty words; they say great things but don't follow through. When leaders don't do what they've promised, it leads to distrust and disillusionment. Dutiful leaders are dependable and have a strong sense of responsibility; they are accountable for their commitments, no matter how difficult.

Harry Truman was born on May 8, 1884 and grew up in Missouri as the eldest son of a hard-working farming family. Family and the farm always came first, and Truman was a dutiful young man who helped with chores and taking care of his younger siblings—brother John Vivian and sister Mary Jane. He was a hard-working student who loved books and hoped to go to college, but his family's needs came first, and college demanded too much time and money. Truman also dreamed of one day becoming a soldier and hoped to attend West Point Naval Academy, but his poor eyesight meant that this dream was also out of reach. After graduating from high school in 1901 Truman tried a few odd jobs, including that of a bank clerk in Kansas City, where he worked until 1906 when his commitment to his family brought him back home to help on the farm.

Truman worked on the family farm for the next decade, but he never gave up his dream of becoming a soldier and serving his country. He enlisted in the National Guard—reportedly passing the eye exam by memorizing the eye chart ahead of time—and was sworn into regular army service as a member of the 129th Field Artillery Regiment in the summer of 1916. Upon the United States' entry into the First World War, Truman's regiment was sent to France, where he was quickly promoted to captain and put in charge of Battery D, 129th Field Artillery Regiment, Thirty-Fifth Division. Truman took his responsibility to his country and to his men very seriously, and thanks to his alert and effective leadership, he led his battery through fierce combat without a single casualty.

After the war, Truman married his longtime sweetheart, Bess, and opened a haberdashery in Kansas City with a war buddy. At first business was good, but soon a recession took its toll on the community and fewer people could afford to buy new clothes and accessories, causing the store to go under after just a couple years. Despite a heavy weight of debt, Truman refused to declare bankruptcy, and instead dutifully toiled for many years to pay off his share of the debt. Moving on from the failed business, Truman chose to use his administrative and leadership skills in another area—the world of politics. Truman began by serving as a judge on the Jackson County Court, and then in 1935 he became a U.S. senator, a position he held for the next ten years.

During the presidential election of 1944 there was much speculation among political pundits about the declining health of incumbent president, Franklin D. Roosevelt. As the Democratic Party geared up for the nomination of their vice-presidential candidate, inevitable debate arose over which candidate would serve as the best running-mate during the election and also prove most capable in the event that he were to be called upon to "succeed the throne." In the end, the nomination fell to a man who had never sought it—Senator Harry S. Truman.

When questioned by a reporter about why he was not seeking the vice-presidential nomination (and potentially, the presidency), Truman, shaking his head, responded: "Hell, I don't want to be president."[1] Truman had no aspirations to become president, and he saw the vice presidency as a position of honor, not action; he preferred his seat in the Senate, where he was very active and felt like he could make a difference. Nonetheless, when pressured by Party leaders and the president himself, Truman felt obliged to accept the nomination, joining Roosevelt on the Democratic ticket. Together they went on to easily win the election, and on a cold January morning in 1945, Truman was sworn in as the thirty-fourth vice president of the United States.

As vice president, Truman experienced little contact with or communication from President Roosevelt. As he had expected, he was left to function in a mostly honorary role. Truman did his best to make the most of the situation, dutifully presiding over the Senate and using his new position to try to improve relations between Congress and the White House. However, unbeknownst to him, Truman was about to become considerably more involved in the affairs of the nation.

On the afternoon of April 12, 1945, Truman received an urgent summons to the White House, where Eleanor Roosevelt revealed that her husband was dead. When the stunned Truman asked the widowed First Lady what he could do for her, she responded, "No Harry, is there anything we can do for you? For you are the one in trouble now."[2] Having served as vice president for less than three months, Truman knew she was right. He said of that moment, "I felt like the moon, the stars and all the planets had fallen on me."[3] Even so, his shock and sense of impending doom did not sway his commitment and determination to fulfill his responsibilities. During a somber ceremony just a few hours later, Truman took the presidential oath and assumed his new duties as President of the United States.

UNDAUNTED - not giving way to fear; undismayed, intrepid, resolute, steadfast, undiscouraged.

Strong and successful leaders are not easily daunted, swayed, or deterred. They are firm and decisive, able to hold their ground and make difficult decisions regardless of opposition. Undaunted leaders remain steadfast, and persevere in the face of adversity, allowing them to lead with confidence and equanimity.

Unlike most other men who have held that position, Truman had neither aspired nor planned for the presidency. But despite his initial shock upon being thrust into the executive office, Truman did not falter, quickly gaining his footing as the new leader of the nation. During his time serving in World War I Truman had proven himself capable of crisis leadership, thinking clearly and effectively while leading a team under extreme pressure. His successful leadership during the war bolstered Truman's confidence and earned the respect of his men. His wartime leadership experience proved invaluable more than twenty-five years later as he once again faced a war—this time as the leader of a nation.

Truman was suddenly the new Commander in Chief, faced with the responsibility of guiding the nation to the long-awaited end of the war. Though he had a decade of experience in local government and another decade of experience in the federal government, Truman had relatively no foreign policy experience when he became president. Having served as vice president for only eighty-two days, Truman had very little contact with President Roosevelt, and he had never been briefed on any of the secret war efforts that the president had undertaken. Nonetheless, Truman remained undaunted. In his first several weeks in office the new president was briefed extensively on the U.S. war efforts—particularly the top-secret Manhattan Project: the development of the atomic bomb.

Truman's fateful decision to authorize the use of atomic bombs against Japan remains controversial to this day. Regardless of whether waging nuclear war was right or wrong, a necessary measure or a ruthless blow, the decision was one that required unquestionable fortitude and determination. He did not make the decision lightly, carefully considering and debating the alternatives over a period of several months. Ultimately, the bombing of Hiroshima and Nagasaki did result in Japanese surrender, and by the end of the summer of 1945 Truman had successfully guided the United States to the end of World War II.

The challenges of war were soon replaced by new difficulties, as the president was tasked with overseeing the difficult economic transition from wartime to peacetime. Faced with shortages, inflation, and labor unrest—all while trying to fill the shoes of his extremely popular predecessor—Truman persevered. He exhibited steadfast determination and carefully made and executed decisions as he tackled these enormous challenges. Thanks to his efforts and overall performance in the context of the times, Truman is generally considered by historians to be among the top U.S. Presidents of all time.[4]

Though he had not initially sought the presidency that was thrust upon him, when it came time to campaign for the 1948 election, Truman was committed. With three and a half years under his belt, Truman knew he had what it took to lead a nation, and he believed he still could do much for America. However, due to divisions within his party, Truman's prospects for election were dim, and political pundits predicted his defeat. Nevertheless, Truman remained undaunted, embarking on an energetic "whistle-stop" campaign across the country. On Election Day, November 2, 1948, American voters went to the polls. Late that evening experts were still predicting Truman's defeat, and the *Chicago Tribune* famously printed the headline "Dewey Defeats Truman" on the November 3 front page. It wasn't until the next morning that Truman and the rest of the world learned that his steadfast perseverance had paid off. In a stunning upset Truman was elected on his own merit as the thirty-third President of the United States.

⌐◦✦◦¬

EFFECTIVE - focusing on and accomplishing that which is most important; making good use of resources; productive, efficient, capable, competent, skillful.

Truly effective leaders focus on pursuing and achieving their most important goals. They place more value on the quality of performance than on quantity of work done. Efficient and competent, effective leaders make good use of their resources and get a lot done, while identifying and focusing on highest priorities and leading their people to achieve what matters most.

In each leadership role that Truman held during his lifetime, he took what resources and people he had available to him, and worked hard to develop and improve them. He tried always to use his position of influence and leadership to make a lasting positive impact, and he earned respect and admiration for his skillful management.

While serving with the National Guard during World War I, Truman was stationed at Camp Doniphan in Fort Sill, Oklahoma for training. In addition to his duties training with his battery, Truman was tasked with running the regiment's canteen. Truman's administrative and financial acumen helped him to run an effective and successful canteen, which was one of a kind among the other canteens in the division, most of which were shut down due to financial problems. When his regiment was sent overseas to engage in combat, Truman was put in command of Battery D, which, having a reputation for being unruly and ineffective, was known as "Dizzy D." Truman's effective leadership won the respect and loyalty of his troops, and he soon transformed the battery into an exemplary unit that performed admirably through the end of the war.

In the years following the war, one of Truman's war buddies introduced him to the politics of Jackson County, Missouri. Truman campaigned and was elected, serving first as a county judge and later as the presiding judge. While in office he sought to help the community, and was able to bring about many significant improvements. One such improvement was the building of more than two hundred miles of paved roads, a huge benefit to the community, especially farmers who transported their goods from farm to market.

Years later, as a U.S. senator, through his habits of hard work, self-discipline and honesty, Truman proved himself to also be a capable and effective congressman. Judicious and efficient in his handling of the Special Committee Investigating National Defense, known as "The Truman Committee," he helped to expose fraud and reduce waste in the U.S. military, saving the country billions of dollars. Truman went on to carry this practice of efficient, effective management with him into the vice presidency and ultimately the presidency.

~⟨☯⟩~

VIRTUOUS - possessing a strong sense of morality; honest, principled, upright, just, fair-minded.

Not only does ethical and moral behavior help keep leaders and their followers out of trouble, but it also lays a foundation of trustworthiness critical for honest communication and relationship building. Virtuous leaders with a reputation of integrity and of being fair-minded receive greater opportunities and ultimately go further than those deemed untrustworthy or unprincipled.

Truman was a man of moral principles. Historians rank Truman among the top three U.S. Presidents to have pursued equal justice for all.[5] Truman believed and stated that, "All Americans, whatever their job, or whatever their income—wherever they live or whatever their race or creed—are entitled to a good education, good medical care and a decent place to live."[6] As president, Truman did more to advance the cause of civil rights than any of his predecessors since Abraham Lincoln, fighting to end racial discrimination in voting, jobs, education, housing and the military.

Truman always endeavored to lead with integrity. His early political career was somewhat tainted by connections to Kansas City's corrupt political boss, the infamous "Boss Tom" Pendergast, who, as the uncle of one of Truman's war buddies, had helped Truman get started in Jackson County. Despite his connections to the Pendergast machine, Truman gained a reputation for honesty. As he advanced politically, Truman continued to surprise his colleagues, gradually overcoming his association with Pendergast by demonstrating sincerity and personal integrity.

Never a fan of excuses, throughout his life Truman took responsibility for his decisions and his actions as a leader. The famous sign that reads "The Buck Stops Here!" sat atop Truman's desk during his presidency, symbolizing his commitment to decisiveness and accountability. Truman's sense of duty, dauntless fortitude, effective management and fair-mindedness enabled him to shoulder the weight of the presidency with grace, leading the nation through the end of the war and toward a better future. Harry S. Truman may not have originally intended to become president, but once in office, he was a very effective leader.

～◌※◌～

4

DWIGHT D. EISENHOWER
PRESIDENTIAL LIBRARY & MUSEUM
Abilene, Kansas

When I first set foot on the grounds of the Eisenhower Presidential Center in Abilene, Kansas, I was somewhat reminded of a military campus that has a large open area for cadet assembly and training. The twenty-two-acre plot of land is vaguely reminiscent of the United States Military Academy at West Point, where Dwight D. Eisenhower first set out on his long military career more than one hundred years ago. However, instead of barracks, mess halls, and classrooms devoted to the education and training of future leaders, the five buildings that make up the Eisenhower Presidential Center are designed to preserve the legacy of one of America's past leaders—a five star general of the army and the thirty-fourth President of the United States.

With spacious lawns and lots of trees, the complex is an ideal place for a picnic when a break is needed from touring the various buildings. Unlike many of the other presidential libraries and

Spacious grounds of the Eisenhower Presidential Library and Museum

museums, the Eisenhower Presidential Library and the Presidential Museum are housed separately, facing each other across a large grassy square. In the center of the square is an eleven-foot bronze statue of the general, set atop a granite base inscribed with quotations from Eisenhower's military and political careers. As I strolled across the campus, I admired the stately buildings built from native Kansas limestone and marveled at the modest two-story home where Eisenhower grew up with his parents and five brothers.

My first stop was the museum, a two-story building filled with amazing history. I slowly made my way through the exhibits, studying displays that tell the story of America during both world wars and the years of peace to follow. I learned how a man who hated the violence of war rose to lead his country through one of the worst conflicts in history and into a much longed-for period of peace. I read about Eisenhower's childhood in Abilene and how he learned the value of hard work at an early age. I perused his family photos and history and tracked his military career from a West Point cadet in 1911 to a five star general in 1944 and beyond. I was reminded of President Eisenhower's global diplomacy, his role in civil rights, his championing of the Interstate Highway System, and the years of peace he so passionately waged.

Statue of General Eisenhower, "The Champion of Peace"

A few hours later I left the museum with a much greater understanding of the major world events and national challenges Eisenhower faced during his life and presidency. I spent the next several minutes breathing in the warm summer air and reflecting on the significant period of history I had just experienced. I then made my way across the complex, pausing to admire the large bronze statue of Eisenhower, the "Champion of Peace," and then stopping to pay my respects at his final resting place inside a little chapel called the "Place of Meditation." The afternoon sunshine streamed through stained glass windows, and colorful rays of light shone upon the tombstones of America's thirty-fourth President and First Lady. I took a few moments to quietly reflect on their lives and to meditate on the words of wisdom inscribed on the surrounding walls.

My tour of the Eisenhower Presidential Center concluded with a look inside the presidential library, a visit to the five memorial pylons at the eastern end of the grounds, and a fascinating tour through the house where Eisenhower grew up. Six hours after my arrival, I drove away with a new understanding and a rekindled respect and admiration for one of my nation's greatest leaders.

Exhibit depicting details of World War II

Military uniforms and photographs from World War II

Did You Know?

As a mischievous cadet at West Point, Eisenhower and a fellow cadet once took an order to appear in "full-dress coats" literally— showing up wearing their dress coats... and nothing else!

**Display featuring sculpture and photograph of
famous Time's Square kiss on V-J Day**

Exhibit depicting Eisenhower's first presidential campaign

Did You Know?
Though he personally never had the chance to fight in combat, Dwight Eisenhower trained troops as a young officer during World War I and commanded the Allied forces during World War II—the only U.S. President to serve in both world wars.

Exhibit featuring widespread peace and prosperity in 1950s America

Eisenhower's boyhood home

Did You Know?

Dwight Eisenhower is one of only five men to ever hold the rank of five-star general of the army.

Five stone pylons memorializing Eisenhower's life and accomplishments

"The Place of Meditation," site of Eisenhower's final resting place

Did You Know?

President Eisenhower named the famous presidential retreat, Camp David, after his grandson. It had previously been called "Shangri-La" by former president Franklin D. Roosevelt.

The gravesite of Dwight and Mamie Eisenhower

WHEN YOU VISIT...
DON'T MISS THESE:

- The Eisenhower Statue, "Champion of Peace"
- Tour of Eisenhower boyhood home
- World War II gallery
- Mamie Eisenhower gallery
- President Eisenhower's farewell speech and warning about the "Military-Industrial Complex"
- Exhibits depicting "The American Dream"
- Personal Diplomacy exhibit
- The Eisenhowers' final resting place within The Place of Meditation

To see many more photos—in full color—please visit
www.presidentialleadershipbook.com/dwight-eisenhower/photos

"A people that values its privileges above its principles soon loses both."

"Leadership is the art of getting someone else to do something you want done because he wants to do it."

"Pull the string, and it will follow wherever you wish. Push it, and it will go nowhere at all."

DWIGHT EISENHOWER
Dedicated, Diplomatic, and *Judicious*

FULL NAME: Dwight David Eisenhower
LIFESPAN: 78 years (1890 – 1969)
TERM: 34th President (R) 1953 – 1961

Dwight D. Eisenhower, affectionately known as "Ike," was born in 1890 in Denison, Texas, and spent his youth in the humble farming community of Abilene, Kansas. He grew up to become a national hero, serving as an illustrious five-star general during World War II. No doubt the leadership lessons he learned during his more than forty years of service in the army prepared him for his position as the thirty-fourth President of the United States.

DEDICATED - wholly committed to an ideal, cause or goal; focused, earnest, determined, persevering.

Leaders who are truly dedicated to a cause and to their followers will persevere in their commitment with fierce determination and enthusiasm. Dedicated leaders believe in what they do and are passionate about what they're trying to accomplish.

After graduating high school in 1909, Eisenhower toiled twelve hours a day, seven days a week at Belle Springs Creamery for two years in order to help pay his brother Edgar's college tuition. The strong work ethic and dedication that Eisenhower demonstrated during this time remained one of his most valuable assets throughout his life. In 1911, Eisenhower left the creamery to pursue a new line of work; after winning appointment through a competitive examination, he entered the U.S. Military Academy at West Point, New York.

Eisenhower graduated from West Point in 1915 and set out on the long and often difficult journey of advancing his military career. He wasn't deployed during World War I and never had the opportunity to fight in combat, serving instead in relatively undistinguished roles over the next two and a half decades. Despite his seemingly stagnant career, Eisenhower remained dedicated to the army and continued to follow his sense of duty and responsibility.

In the 1920s Eisenhower was stationed in Panama, where he became acquainted with General Fox Conner. General Conner was a highly intelligent and respected officer who had served as the Chief of Operations for the American Expeditionary Force in France during the First World War. General Conner, who was especially talented as an army strategist and military historian, took a keen interest in Eisenhower, whom he felt had great potential. Over the next three years, he privately tutored Eisenhower on military history, strategy, and leadership, and gave him an extensive reading list to supplement this informal but invaluable education.

Thanks to the influence of General Conner, in 1925 Eisenhower secured an appointment to the Command and General Staff College at Fort Leavenworth, Kansas. He went on to graduate first in his class of 245 officers, an accomplishment that helped to advance his career another small but significant step.

Eisenhower slowly rose up the ranks, serving in increasingly difficult roles—the most challenging being his seven years of service under General Douglas MacArthur. By this time Eisenhower had proven himself to be a valuable officer who was intelligent, articulate, and extremely hard working. As such, he became an indispensable aide and advisor to General MacArthur. The general's vainglorious personality and overbearing attitude often tested the limits of Eisenhower's patience, but he continued to persevere. Though he often disagreed with the decisions and behavior of his superior officer, Eisenhower remained a loyal soldier, serving under MacArthur until the outbreak of World War II.

With the beginning of war in Europe and the possibility of U.S. involvement, Eisenhower chose to return to the United States from where he was stationed in the Philippines, bringing his service under MacArthur to a close and marking a new stage in his military career. The next few years afforded Eisenhower the opportunity to begin actively training troops for the looming war. This new role revealed Eisenhower's latent leadership ability and his talent for military tactics and strategic planning. Having thus far persevered for more than twenty undistinguished years in the army, often serving in obscure administrative roles, Eisenhower's career finally began to look promising. He rose in rank—within just a few short years—to become a senior officer, and ultimately the Supreme Commander of the Allied Expeditionary Forces and a five-star general of the army. It had been a long, slow journey, but Eisenhower's dedication and perseverance ultimately paid off.

DIPLOMATIC – skilled in handling delicate matters and in dealing well with people; tactful, charming.

Without question, diplomacy is a very useful skill for any leader. Diplomatic leaders are perceptive to individual perspectives and attitudes, and have a knack for pinpointing needs and striking compromise. With effective diplomacy, leaders can skillfully mediate conflict and tactfully handle even the most challenging personalities—a truly critical leadership asset.

Decades before becoming a senior officer, while he was an upperclassman at West Point, Eisenhower had a brief encounter with another cadet that became one of his defining experiences: A freshman cadet, called a plebe, accidentally collided with Eisenhower in a hallway. Annoyed, Eisenhower decided to take the opportunity to haze the young cadet—a common practice— saying mockingly, "You look like a barber!" The plebe flushed with embarrassment and quietly said, "I was a barber, sir." Taken aback, Eisenhower felt a sudden pang of guilt at humiliating the young man, and quickly returned to his room where he told his roommate that he would never haze another plebe again, saying, "I've just done something stupid and unforgiveable. I managed to make a man ashamed of the work he did to earn a living."[1] After that, Eisenhower strove to never humiliate, embarrass, or demean another person, no matter how annoyed he became. This personal resolution developed into a keen sense of diplomacy that served him exceedingly well as he slowly rose in military rank.

The twenty-five years between Eisenhower's graduation from West Point and the outbreak of World War II served not only to develop his knowledge of military strategy and affairs, but also his remarkable conflict resolution skills. By the time he became a general, Eisenhower had decades of experience in the political jungle of the military. His extensive experience working with high-level officers had helped Eisenhower further develop his characteristic diplomacy, and he was able to skillfully smooth over disputes and mediate conflicting interests and demands. He had learned from his mentor, General Fox Conner, the essential subtleties of securing cooperation with his allies—a task that often proved more difficult than the rather straightforward matter of dealing with enemies. These skills proved indispensable to Eisenhower as a top military leader and later as the president.

Overall, Eisenhower was great with people. He had a strong temper, but he learned to keep it in check, and outwardly he was charming and good-natured. He had a vibrant personality, outstanding reputation, and strong personal presence, while remaining unassuming and modest. With an easy grin and piercing blue eyes, Eisenhower inspired trust and confidence in those with whom he interacted—a truly indispensable leadership quality.

⌐◠✢◠⌐

JUDICIOUS – having and exercising good judgment; intelligent, strategic, perceptive, wise, sensible, prudent, pragmatic.

Judicious leaders make well-thought-out decisions and plan for long-term results. Strategic and pragmatic, they don't always pursue the most obvious, less difficult course, but rather the course that fits their best judgment. While not immune to mistakes or poor decisions, their careful thinking and astute observations help judicious leaders succeed again and again.

E isenhower valued honesty and forthrightness, but he was also a poker player and knew how to play a hidden hand. As the Cold War escalated, President Eisenhower learned the importance of showing a confident and optimistic face as a leader, while carefully working behind the scenes to prevent nuclear disaster. He realized that careful strategy and subterfuge were sometimes necessary when protecting national interests. Eisenhower's vice president, Richard Nixon, once described him as "devious—in the best sense of the word."

In order to not reveal sensitive information to the press, President Eisenhower sometimes evaded questions by adopting a strategy of "saying nothing while using a lot of words." Once, when his press secretary, James Hagerty, expressed concern about how Eisenhower should respond to certain questions during an upcoming press conference, Eisenhower responded, "Don't worry, Jim. If that comes up, I'll just confuse them."[2] Eisenhower was smart enough to know that he didn't always need to look smart; he was comfortable with sometimes bearing the image of an "old bumbler" if it meant protecting the interests of the nation he led.

Eisenhower's poker skill had served him well as a young officer—he used his winnings to help pay for his army uniforms. The talents that made him a good poker player also proved to be assets throughout his life; his mathematic abilities and powers of observation proved invaluable to Eisenhower as a military strategist and as a political leader. Eisenhower was always a perceptive man, and throughout his life he demonstrated a knack for making astute character assessments and personnel decisions—a critical asset that proved to be one of his greatest leadership skills.

It was Eisenhower's reputation as an assertive and sharp officer who wasn't afraid to assume responsibility that caught the attention of General George C. Marshall at the beginning of World War II. General Marshall's request for Eisenhower's presence in Washington, DC just days after the attack on Pearl Harbor was the beginning of the series of moves that culminated in Eisenhower's promotion to General of the Army in 1944. In turn, Eisenhower's service as a five-star general during World War II caught the attention of the nation. People appreciated his unassuming manner and respected his masterful leadership ability, developed and honed over the course of his extensive career. After his return to the U.S. following the war, it was no surprise when people began to urge their national hero to run for president.

Though he often received it, Eisenhower did not require the adoration of the public; he was comfortable with making unpopular decisions or allowing poor public perception of his actions if it helped the cause of the military or the good of the nation. As both a military officer and as the president, Eisenhower often chose to give others plausible deniability, accepting the full brunt of public scrutiny and criticism for difficult decisions. He was also not hesitant to redirect credit that he was due when he felt doing so would be more beneficial in the big picture.

As he exhibited throughout his military and presidential career, Eisenhower was intelligent and pragmatic, making well-thought-out decisions and planning for long-term results. He thought carefully about the consequences of his decisions and actions, and always strove to consider different viewpoints. Many of his contemporaries never realized the full extent of Eisenhower's intelligence and pragmatism; only through the lens of history has his judicious leadership been fully revealed.

Beloved and renowned throughout the world, President Eisenhower was just as popular in the public eye when he left office as when he entered it. Every year from 1952 to 1960 Eisenhower captured the top spot on Gallup's poll of America's most admired men. As an elder statesman, he went on to capture the title again in both 1968 and 1969. Also among his impressive achievements is a long list of awards and recognition from more than thirty different countries. His dedication, diplomacy and sound judgment helped make him into one of the greatest leaders of the twentieth century. Without question, much can be learned from the leadership of this five-star general of the army and thirty-fourth President of the United States.

5

JOHN F. KENNEDY
PRESIDENTIAL LIBRARY & MUSEUM
Boston, Massachusetts

The John F. Kennedy Presidential Library and Museum, located on a ten-acre park on Columbia Point in Boston, overlooks the sea that the thirty-fifth U.S. President loved so much. Kennedy, who was born in the Boston suburb of Brookline, Massachusetts, received a sailboat named *Victura* for his fifteenth birthday. Kennedy's love for the sea and his beloved sailboat never faded. With *Victura* he won sailing competitions as a young man, taught his wife, Jackie, to sail, and enjoyed much needed reprieves from the challenges of the Oval Office while president. Now the sailboat that meant so much to the young politician resides on the grounds of the library and museum that preserves his legacy.

The first thing that drew my attention when I arrived at the John F. Kennedy Presidential Library and Museum was the imposing 125-foot concrete tower, which I later learned houses offices and the archives. Connected to the tower are exhibit halls, theaters, and

View of Boston skyline across the harbor from the library and museum

a spectacular glass atrium within which hangs a giant American flag. Outside the walls of the library and museum is a beautiful view of the harbor and the Boston skyline. As a salty breeze blew off the water and the sunshine fell warm on my back, I could feel the alluring tug of the sea that drew Kennedy into the navy and continued to call to him throughout his life.

After admiring the view and the striking architecture of the building, I made my way inside and began my tour. I perused exhibits that told the story of Kennedy's family heritage and upbringing. I learned about Kennedy's service in the navy and the selfless courage that made him a hero when his vessel, PT-109, was sunk and his crew stranded. I paused to examine photographs from his wedding and pictures of his young family. I reminisced in front of exhibits representing the campaign trail and a mock storefront with its displays of appliances and products from the sixties. I marveled at how close America came to nuclear war during the Cuban missile crisis, and I silently expressed my gratitude for the actions Kennedy took to avert it. I explored the space exhibit and recalled that proud moment when Kennedy's dream of putting a man on the moon was finally fulfilled nearly eight years after his death.

Near the end of my tour I entered a dark alcove where I soberly

Giant American flag hanging in the tall glass atrium

reflected on that fateful date, November 22, 1963, and I remembered exactly where I was and how I reacted when I heard the news. Standing in the alcove, I once again watched Walter Cronkite's familiar face lined with grief as he made the official announcement, "From Dallas, Texas, the flash—apparently official: President Kennedy died at one p.m. central standard time, two o'clock eastern standard time… some thirty-eight minutes ago."[1] Watching that historic news story unfold, I empathized with the shock that reverberated around the nation, and I again admired Jackie Kennedy's dignity and courage in the face of such tragedy.

Moving on from the memorial gallery, I entered the large glass atrium and craned my neck to view the huge twenty-six-by-forty-five-foot American flag suspended from the ceiling. As I marveled at the immense flag and the structure that houses it, I reflected on the legacy that President Kennedy left behind. In his own words, "A man may die, nations may rise and fall, but an idea lives on."[2] Indeed, the ideas that John F. Kennedy shared with the world do live on—through the lives of each person who remembers and honors his life and leadership.

Typewriter similar to that used by Kennedy while at Harvard

Coconut shell bearing a message from Lt. Kennedy during PT-109 incident

Did You Know?
John F. Kennedy, who often went by the nickname "Jack," was the second of nine children.

Jackie's camera from her days as the "Inquiring Camera Girl"

Storefront and merchandise typical of the early 1960s

Did You Know?

During Kennedy's administration John Glenn became the first American to orbit the earth.

Re-creation of a Kennedy presidential campaign office

Reproduction of studio where first televised debate took place

Did You Know?

Prior to their famous battle for the presidency in 1960, John F. Kennedy and Richard Nixon were friends, having served together in Congress for several years.

Large presidential seal flanked by American and presidential flags

Hallway and alcoves filled with historical exhibits and artifacts

Did You Know?
The Kennedys' second son, Patrick Bouvier, was born during his father's third year as President, but tragically died within two days due to premature birth. His father was assassinated less than four months later.

Kennedy's sailboat, *Victura*, outside of the library and museum

WHEN YOU VISIT...
DON'T MISS THESE:

- Scenic walk around the building and the view of Boston harbor and skyline
- JFK's sailboat, *Victura*
- Large American flag hanging within glass atrium
- Exhibits depicting Kennedy's naval service and the PT-109 incident
- Campaign trail and election gallery
- Reproduction of studio where the famous first televised presidential debate took place
- Exhibits depicting Jackie Kennedy's life and pursuits
- Exhibits featuring America's space program
- Alcove and displays featuring JFK's close working relationship with his brother Bobby Kennedy
- Replica of JFK's Oval Office desk and rocking chair
- Dark alcove somberly remembering JFK's assassination

To see many more photos—in full color—please visit
www.presidentialleadershipbook.com/john-f-kennedy/photos

"The problems of the world cannot possibly be solved by skeptics or cynics whose horizons are limited by the obvious realities. We need men who can dream of things that never were, and ask 'why not?'"

"Those who dare to fail miserably can achieve greatly."

"There are risks and costs to a program of action. But they are far less than the long-range risks and costs of comfortable inaction."

JOHN F. KENNEDY
Charismatic, Eloquent, Inspiring and *Courageous*

FULL NAME: John Fitzgerald Kennedy
LIFESPAN: 46 years (1917 – 1963)
TERM: 35th President (D) 1961 – 1963

The first president to be born in the twentieth century, John F. Kennedy was also the youngest man and the first Roman Catholic to be elected to the office of U.S. President. The young politician represented a new generation and a season of change, and he possessed a kind of magnetism that resonated with people around the world. Not only was Kennedy the youngest man to be elected president, he was also the youngest president to die; the charismatic young president was senselessly shot down on the streets of Dallas, Texas, at the age of forty-six—just 1,036 days into his presidency.

CHARISMATIC - possessing a personal quality that others find attractive; smooth, charming, magnetic, influential.

Charisma may be one of the most important leadership traits that separate the good from the great. The most successful leaders usually demonstrate charisma. Charismatic leaders have a certain magnetism about them, a charming personality and appeal that less successful leaders lack. Leaders who possess great charisma possess great influence; their ability to attract and compel followers enables them to accomplish remarkable things.

Kennedy had dashing good looks and irrepressible charm with which he wooed the ladies, and ultimately, the nation. The second of nine children, Kennedy was born into a privileged family, and though he grew up during the Great Depression, he was shielded from its devastating effects. Free from the oppressive poverty experienced by so many of his countrymen, Kennedy was a carefree, energetic, athletic, and popular young man. Though he suffered from various ailments throughout his life, Kennedy had a robust personality and competitive spirit that effectively concealed his poor health. As a student at Harvard University in the late 1930s, Kennedy enjoyed immense popularity as a fun, handsome young man with a radiant smile.

After college, Kennedy enlisted in the navy, where he was assigned to command a patrol torpedo boat in the South Pacific. On a dark night in 1943, his boat was demolished in a collision with a Japanese destroyer. Kennedy's courageous actions as he struggled to get the surviving members of his crew to safety earned him a medal for courageous leadership. His nationally publicized heroism earned him an even higher status in the hearts and minds of his fellow Americans.

Kennedy entered the political arena in 1946, campaigning for a seat in the U.S. Congress. His charm, good looks, military heroism, and family of influence were a winning combination, and Kennedy went on to serve three terms in the House. He secured another substantial victory in 1952 by winning a coveted seat in the U.S. Senate. Kennedy then made a bid for the vice-presidential spot on the democratic ticket in 1956. Though this campaign was unsuccessful, it prepared and positioned him for his next one—this time as a presidential candidate.

When it came to his hard fought victory during the presidential election of 1960, historians believe a key factor to his triumph was the televised presidential debate where viewers saw Kennedy as a charming, relaxed, handsome, and healthy-looking man versus his pallid, tense and uncomfortable-looking rival, Richard Nixon. Throughout his campaign Kennedy turned on the charm and engaged with voters. When election results were in, a razor-thin margin separated the two candidates, with Kennedy declared the winner. No doubt his charisma and strength of presence played a large part in his victory.

～⌒⁀⌒～

ELOQUENT - having and exercising the power of articulate, forceful and appropriate speech; expressive, moving.

Eloquent leaders understand and leverage the power of effective communication. Armed with a strong vocabulary, practiced delivery, and powerful points, eloquent leaders can use words to inspire their followers and accomplish significant goals. Eloquent leaders are able to effectively articulate critical instructions, important priorities, broad visions, and new ideas to those whom they lead.

Though he was a mostly average student in high school and college, Kennedy had a way with words, and he worked hard in the subjects that greatly interested him—English, history, and government. Even as a youth Kennedy expressed a growing interest in current events; he enjoyed a daily subscription to the *New York Times* as an adolescent, and while in college he spent a summer touring Europe and learning about world affairs. As a senior at Harvard University in 1939, Kennedy's eloquence and intellectual potential was revealed when he wrote his thesis about England's lack of preparedness on the brink of World War II. Kennedy went on to publish the well-written paper as a book in 1940, called *Why England Slept*. Years later as a senator, Kennedy published a second book,

Profiles in Courage, which became a bestseller and won the Pulitzer Prize for Biography in 1957.

Kennedy had considered becoming a full-time writer or teacher, and after college and the navy he spent a short time as a journalist, further developing his skill with words. Though he was still intrigued by politics and current events, it was really John's older brother, Joe, who had been the Kennedy boy with the high political aspirations and distinct potential for following their father into public office. But when Joe was tragically killed during the war, the Kennedy family's political legacy shifted to rest on the shoulders of the second son, John, who soon began pursuing a future in public office.

As he began campaigning for political office, John Kennedy's smooth and persuasive communication skills aided him tremendously. Kennedy made a point to study famous speeches by great American communicators such as Abraham Lincoln and Franklin D. Roosevelt. Artistically imitating the terse, poignant style of these renowned orators, Kennedy delivered masterful speeches that have left a lasting impression on the nation and on the world.

꒰ꗥ꒱

INSPIRING - possessing the ability to stimulate, influence and arouse others to action; exciting, visionary, engaging, compelling.

There is no motivating factor as powerful as true inspiration. While reward-based or fear-based motivation yields limited results, inspiration is longer lasting, more deeply rooted, and internally driven rather than externally driven. Inspiring leaders are able to stir the hearts and minds of their followers, compelling them to action with greater loyalty and enthusiasm than achieved by any other sort of motivator.

Kennedy was not only gifted in articulate public address, but he also possessed an innate ability to cast a vision and express concepts that resonated in the hearts and minds of the American people. With a few carefully chosen words delivered in vivid style, Kennedy could inspire millions and spur crowds of listeners on to action.

In his speeches, Kennedy painted an alluring picture of America's future, stirring up patriotism and passion in the hearts of a new generation of Americans. He boldly declared that the old era of politics and government was ending and that the old ways would no longer do; "It is a time, in short, for a new generation of leadership."[3] He spoke also of a "New Frontier"—the frontier of the 1960s. During his presidential campaign Kennedy delivered a poignant description of this exciting New Frontier: "The frontier of unknown opportunities and perils, the frontier of unfulfilled hopes and threats... Beyond that frontier are uncharted areas of science and space, unsolved problems of peace and war, unconquered pockets of ignorance and prejudice, unanswered questions of poverty and surplus."[4]

Kennedy challenged the American status quo, calling upon all Americans to take personal responsibility for the future of their nation. Upon accepting the Democratic nomination for the presidency, he explained, "The New Frontier of which I speak is not a set of promises—it is a set of challenges. It sums up not what I intend to offer the American people, but what I intend to ask of them."[5] Months later, during his inaugural address, the new president uttered his most famous line: "Ask not what your country can do for you; ask what you can do for your country!"[6] This sentiment of bold new leadership and active citizenry permeated Kennedy's presidency and inspired the nation.

President Kennedy was beloved and admired by more than just the citizens of the United States. When he arrived for a speech at the Rudolph Wilde Platz in Berlin on June 26, 1963, hundreds of thousands of Berliners received Kennedy with a standing ovation that lasted several minutes. His speech that day, among dozens more, is still remembered, quoted, and cherished around the world.

In addition to his rousing speeches, Kennedy also stirred hearts and minds with his ideas, actions and legislative proposals. One such Kennedy program was the Peace Corp, established by his executive order on March 1, 1961, and approved by Congress by the end of the year. This exciting global outreach program inspired, equipped, and commissioned American volunteers to aid in the educational and agricultural development of third world countries. In the more than fifty years since Kennedy's dream became a reality, the Peace Corp has served to promote the spread of democracy, peace, and global good will, further solidifying America's powerful international reputation.

~◠◡◠~

COURAGEOUS – able and willing to face difficulty, pain, danger, etc., without or despite fear; brave, daring, bold, intrepid, resolved, determined, fearless.

Courageous leadership takes boldness, fortitude, and steadfast resolve. Courageous leaders possess a willingness to accept risk, endure consequences, and withstand adversity. When bolstered by unflagging courage, leaders accomplish greater things and inspire courage in those they lead.

Though his life was tragically cut short, throughout his ascension to the presidency and during his relatively brief time in office, Kennedy faced an array of challenges that tested his strength and resolve. Coming from a privileged background did not mean that his life was all smooth sailing or that he did not face adversity. Throughout his life Kennedy faced hardship with fortitude, and he left behind a legacy of both military and political courage.

Prior to his political career, Kennedy became famous for his military heroism during World War II. The facts remain unclear in regard to the events of that fateful night in the South Pacific leading up to when Navy Lieutenant John F. Kennedy's PT boat was demolished by a Japanese warship. However, Kennedy's courageous actions immediately following the incident are undisputed. Though he himself was injured, Lieutenant Kennedy towed a badly burned crew member to safety by gripping a strap from the man's life jacket in his teeth while swimming more than three miles to a small island. Over the course of the next several days an exhausted Kennedy made several attempts to locate potential rescuers by swimming to neighboring islands and looking for any signs of U.S. ships. Finally, nearly a week after their boat had been sunk and two of their crew members killed, the crew of PT-109 was rescued after two native islanders delivered a message from Kennedy to a nearby navy outpost. Kennedy received a U.S. Navy and Marine Corp medal for his courage and leadership and was also awarded a Purple Heart for the injuries he incurred during the ordeal.

That same courage and steadfast resolve that sustained Kennedy during the war also saw him through the rough waters of politics. As an Irish-Catholic candidate during an era when a heavily Protestant nation was concerned about the amount of influence the Catholic papacy and diocese might have on a Catholic president, Kennedy faced a significant hurdle in his campaign for the presidency. Undaunted, he faced this challenge head-on with openness and honesty; Kennedy allowed leading Protestant clergy to question his views on church-state relations, providing them with clear, direct answers, and successfully easing the concerns of many voters. In November 1960, John F. Kennedy became the first Catholic to be elected to the United States presidency.

Early in his presidency, Kennedy faced the embarrassment and international fallout resulting from the failed Bay of Pigs invasion. In the aftermath of the botched political coup, launched in hopes of overthrowing Cuba's communist government, young President Kennedy appeared weak and inexperienced. However, rather than crushing him, this failure fueled his resolve. The following year Kennedy went on to deal smoothly with one of the world's most alarming nuclear threats in history—the Cuban missile crisis. After intense deliberation, the Kennedy administration took decisive action, and succeeded in defusing a potentially catastrophic conflict with the communist Soviet Union.

In addition to foreign crisis, Kennedy faced trouble at home as growing unrest among civil rights activists threatened the peace and safety of Americans across the nation. Though initially reluctant to throw his hat in the ring and risk alienating a large segment of his constituents, on June 11, 1963 Kennedy demonstrated his political courage and took a public stand for what he felt was right. During a powerful, televised speech, Kennedy expressed his dismay at how basic American rights and privileges were being denied to citizens of color. He boldly stated, "It ought to be possible for every American to enjoy the privileges of being American, without regard to his race or his color."[7] He entreated the American people to stand with him on this issue, to uphold the constitution and fulfill the promise of freedom for all Americans. It was with this kind of courage, vision, eloquence, and strength of presence that Kennedy led a nation and inspired the world.

6

LYNDON B. JOHNSON
PRESIDENTIAL LIBRARY & MUSEUM
Austin, Texas

Located on thirty acres in the midst of the University of Texas campus in Austin, Texas, the LBJ Presidential Library and Museum was dedicated on May 22, 1971. Since opening its doors more than forty years ago, the library and museum has welcomed hundreds of thousands of visitors. Thanks to its location only a few hours from my home, I have had the privilege of visiting this library and museum several times, always enjoying the experience and gaining new insight into the life and times of the thirty-sixth U.S. President.

On one of my visits, a warm November day a week after Thanksgiving, I spent six hours admiring the unique architecture and taking in all the exhibits, carefully framing and taking hundreds of photos as I toured. The archives and the museum exhibits are housed together in one imposing ten-story structure made of travertine limestone. The building looks like an impenetrable fortress, with

Fountain in front of the LBJ Library and Museum

walls that are eight-feet thick at the bottom and a tenth floor that sits squarely on top, overhanging the rest of the building by fifteen-feet on each side. As I approached the library from the parking lot, I first passed under the LBJ School of Public Affairs, then crossed the large raised plaza surrounding the building. I paused for a moment to watch the gently waving American and Texas flags, which stood near the edge of the plaza and were framed against a vivid blue sky.

As I took photos of the flags and the building, a friendly security guard approached me with a smile. She introduced herself as Verla, and let me know that the fountain located on the lawn adjacent to the plaza would be shut off during the hottest hours of the day to conserve water. If I'd like to photograph it, the window of opportunity was closing. I thanked her graciously and proceeded down to the fountain where I took several great photos before her prediction proved true. After completing my tour around the exterior of the building—including a visit to the small Texas wildflower gardens honoring Lady Bird Johnson—I stepped into the air conditioning and began making my way through the museum. The first display I passed bore these introductory words:

You are invited to embark on a walk through history, the history

Lady Bird Johnson Wildflower Garden

of America through six decades of the twentieth century. They are eventful years of tumult and change. These years—1908 to 1973—are not chosen at random. They are the years that comprise the early life and public career of the thirty-sixth President of the United States of America.[1]

LBJ himself was adamant that his library and museum tell the full story—no glossing over the controversies or depicting him as anything less or more than the fallible man he was. As he put it, "It is all here: the story of our time with the bark off... this library will show the facts, not just the joy and triumphs, but the sorrow and failures too."[2]

Indeed, as I wound my way through the exhibits, delving into American history, I saw LBJ's story "with the bark off." From the little farmhouse on the banks of the Pedernales River where he was born, through his long political career, to his final resting place on his beloved Texas ranch, LBJ's life and legacy is on display for all to see.

I was intrigued by the timeline of LBJ's life set into the context of the times—his childhood during the First World War, his early adulthood during the Great Depression, his congressional career during the Second World War and the years of peace that followed,

Etched magnesium mural depicting stages of LBJ's political career

and his vice presidency and presidency as the civil rights movement exploded across the country and the war in Vietnam worsened. I was especially impressed by the large etched magnesium mural, located underneath the four stories of windows that give visitors a unique peek into the archives. The mural depicts LBJ first as a congressman with President Roosevelt, then as a senator with President Truman, senate majority leader with President Eisenhower, vice president with President Kennedy, and finally as president himself.

On one of my return visits more than a year later, not long after the completion of a major renovation, I was delighted to see the mural still in place under the archives' windows. The rest of the museum featured fascinating new exhibits and interactive displays, which I enjoyed exploring throughout the day. Toward the end of my visit, I received a special, unexpected treat. Thanks to a generous offer from a museum staff member, I had the tremendous privilege of taking a personal tour of a part of the museum I hadn't even known existed—the private presidential suite located on the top floor of the building. I was awed by this private suite, reserved only for LBJ and Lady Bird, and kept secret and off-limits from the general public ever since its construction. I appreciated this special behind-the-scenes tour more than I could express in words—what a perfect way to end

**Exhibit featuring campaign poster and photographs
from LBJ's congressional career**

a fascinating day!

Every time I leave the museum, I have a much greater under-standing and empathy for the challenges President Johnson faced, and a deeper appreciation for his many accomplishments. I admire the honest portrayal of his life and legacy that LBJ insisted upon for his museum. I always walk away more than a little awed by the man who has been described as "bigger than life," who indeed left a legacy much bigger than his own life.

Exhibit depicting the Kennedy-Johnson campaign of 1960

Exhibit featuring news headlines from that fateful day, November 22, 1963

Did You Know?

Lyndon Baines Johnson's wife, Claudia Alta Taylor, went by her nickname "Lady Bird," throughout her life. The Johnsons named their daughters Lynda Bird and Luci Baines, effectively giving their entire family the same initials—"LBJ."

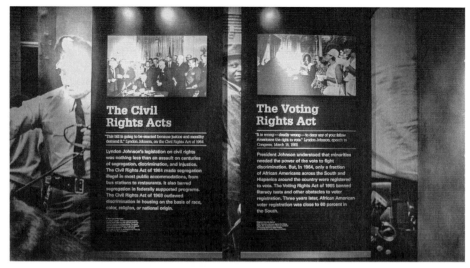

Exhibit depicting civil rights legislation
President Johnson pushed through Congress

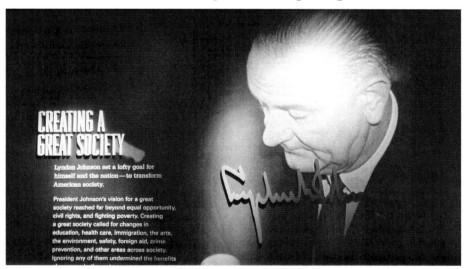

Exhibit depicting LBJ's primary initiative, creating a "Great Society"

Did You Know?

LBJ proposed to Lady Bird on their first date, which was the day after they met. Stunned, Lady Bird initially demurred, but she gave in after ten weeks of courtship when LBJ showed up on her doorstep and suggested they get married immediately. They were married the next day, November 17, 1934, beginning the first day of their thirty-eight year marriage.

Part of an exhibit depicting the details and controversy of the Vietnam War

Exhibit featuring the famous "Johnson Treatment"

Did You Know?
Johnson briefly served as an officer in the navy during World War II while maintaining his seat in the U.S. House of Representatives. Lady Bird ran LBJ's congressional office while he was away.

View of library archives from inside the museum's Great Hall

Display featuring portraits of each U.S. President and First Lady

Did You Know?

Lyndon B. Johnson was one of the tallest presidents in U.S. history, tied with Abraham Lincoln at six feet four inches. LBJ was already six feet three inches tall by the time he graduated high school at the age of fifteen.

Display within museum gift shop that includes candid photo of LBJ howling with his dog while his grandson looks on

WHEN YOU VISIT...
DON'T MISS THESE:

- Small Lady Bird wildflower garden outside of museum
- The impressive view of the library's archives from the museum's Great Hall
- Etched magnesium mural depicting Johnson's political career
- The White House Years gallery featuring items from LBJ's presidency
- The three televisions President Johnson famously watched inside his Oval Office
- The Legacy Gallery
- The Social Justice Gallery
- LBJ's presidential limousine

To see many more photos—in full color—please visit
www.presidentialleadershipbook.com/lyndon-johnson/photos

"There are no problems we cannot solve together, and very few that we can solve by ourselves."

"You aren't learning anything when you're talking."

"We must open the doors of opportunity. But we must also equip our people to walk through those doors."

LYNDON JOHNSON
Driven, Zealous, Shrewd and *Fair-Minded*

FULL NAME: Lyndon Baines Johnson
LIFESPAN: 64 years (1908 – 1973)
TERM: 36th President (D) 1963 – 1969

The name and presidency of Lyndon B. Johnson will forever be associated with the controversy of the Vietnam War, but when reflecting on the thirty-sixth U.S. President, one shouldn't let the dark cloud of war obscure the full picture of his presidency. In the context of the times, President Johnson made significant strides in combating racial discrimination, improving the plight of America's poorest communities, and bringing greater attention and aid to public education.

DRIVEN – compelled to succeed or excel; fiercely motivated, ambitious and determined; possessing strong work ethic; dedicated, focused.

Leaders who are driven are continually in pursuit of greater success. They have their eyes set on a goal, and they utilize every bit of their knowledge and influence to reach that goal. With every goal reached, truly driven leaders set new, bigger and better targets and redirect their energies and passion in pursuit of these new goals.

Lyndon Johnson was one of the hardest working politicians in American history. His passion for and commitment to the job remains legendary. He campaigned tirelessly, and when elected to office, worked with equal dedication and intensity. His strong work ethic and passion for improving the lives and welfare of the American people stemmed from his youth—growing up in depression-era central Texas, where he experienced first-hand the plight of the impoverished.

After graduating high school at the age of fifteen, Johnson worked odd jobs for a few years until deciding to attend Southwest Texas State Teachers College in San Marcus, about fifty miles from where he grew up in Johnson City. Johnson enjoyed and excelled at student teaching, spending a year at a tiny Mexican-American school in Cotulla, Texas where he taught fifth, sixth and seventh grades. Johnson challenged the long-neglected students and brought to the school renewed hope and confidence, earning glowing references.

After a brief but meaningful period as a teacher, Johnson discovered his true calling; he entered politics in 1931 when he became an aide to Congressman Richard Kleberg. After his move to Washington, Johnson's exemplary work ethic propelled him up the political ladder, first securing him an appointment as the Texas Director of the National Youth Administration by President Roosevelt in 1935. He then entered Congress in 1937 by winning the open seat in the House following the death of Texas Representative James P. Buchanan.

As a congressman, Johnson used his position to lobby for legislation that would aid the impoverished and disadvantaged. One of his proudest accomplishments was bringing electrification to rural Texas through the building of dams on the lower Colorado River. Congressman Johnson continued to prove himself in Washington, and after an early unsuccessful run for the Senate in 1941, he went on to win a seat eight years later. Johnson quickly became Senate majority whip and later, minority leader. Then in 1954 the Democrats retook control of the Senate, and the following year, when Johnson was forty-six, the hard-working politician from Texas was elected as one of the youngest and most powerful Senate majority leaders in American history.

In 1960 Johnson made a bid for the White House. Though he was a skillful and powerful politician, Johnson's experience proved to be insufficient in a race against his popular young competitor for the Democratic nomination, John F. Kennedy. Kennedy's youth, charm, military heroism, and influential family easily swept him onto the Democratic ticket on the first ballot. In a politically calculated move, Kennedy offered the vice-presidential spot on the ticket to the tall senator from Texas, and after careful deliberation, Johnson accepted. It was a close-fought race against the Republican Nixon-Lodge ticket, but after election results were in, Kennedy and Johnson were declared the winners, and Johnson became the thirty-seventh vice president of the United States.

ZEALOUS – ardently active, devoted, or diligent; vigorous, energetic, fervent, eager, intense, passionate, dynamic, forceful.

Zealous leaders exude intense passion, concern, or enthusiasm for their cause or goal. When directed toward a worthy cause, a leader's zeal can yield dramatic positive results. Zealous leaders can be dynamic and inspiring, spreading contagious energy and passion among those they lead, and arousing even the most passive followers to effective action.

Johnson's entire life was marked by effective action and energy. He was driven and ambitious, intent on succeeding at whatever he tried, and not easily deterred once he set his mind to something. When it came to campaigning for office and lobbying for legislation, Johnson attacked it with such energy and zeal that he wore out his competition.

After the tragic slaying of President John F. Kennedy in November 1963, Vice President Johnson assumed the presidency. As president, Johnson drove himself and his staff to use every second of his presidency; his signature admonition was, "Do it now. Not next week. Not tomorrow. Not later today. Now."[3] Intolerant of procrastination, inactivity, or—heaven forbid—apathy, Johnson insisted on full commitment and immediate action.

One of President Johnson's aides, Joseph A. Califano, Jr., recalls, "As allies and enemies alike slumped in exhaustion, we saw how LBJ's relentless zeal produced second, third and fourth bursts of energy."[4] Johnson was determined to use the power of public office to mount a massive social revolution, known as the "Great Society," that would give new hope to the disadvantaged.

As both a representative and a senator, Johnson had developed extensive knowledge and experience with the inner workings of Congress, and he possessed a masterful ability to woo and sway his fellow congressmen in his efforts to push legislation through Congress. The energetic Johnson had a talent for balancing straightforward and forceful tactics with gentler, intelligent persuasion. He was assertive yet flattering, forceful yet cajoling; above all, he was persistent and determined to succeed. He carried this dynamic energy with him into his vice presidency and presidency.

SHREWD – very astute and sharp in practical matters; perceptive, discerning, keen, intelligent, savvy, pragmatic.

Shrewd leaders are perceptive and pragmatic. With a clear agenda in mind, they recognize and leverage the smallest of opportunities in every situation, and learn to utilize to their advantage subtle nuances of individual personalities and circumstances. Through their remarkable discernment and keen people skills, shrewd leaders can accomplish the seemingly impossible.

Though Johnson had always had high political aspirations, he had never envisioned becoming president as the result of a national tragedy. Five days after the assassination of John F. Kennedy, the new president somberly told Congress and the American people, "All that I have I would have given gladly not to be standing here today."[5] Nonetheless, standing there he was, suddenly the President of the United States, and Johnson was determined to give his very best to the American people. His practical knowledge of the mechanics of the office and political process, gained from his time in Congress, gave Johnson a foundation to build on. He may have been dismayed by the circumstances of his sudden ascension to the presidency, but he was not unprepared for the challenges of the office.

Johnson astutely realized that providing continuity in the presidency was vital to its success, and he pledged to carry on the torch passed to him by President Kennedy. During his first televised address to a joint session of Congress, Johnson stirred the heart of the nation with his declaration that, "No words are sad enough to express our sense of loss. No words are strong enough to express our determination to continue the forward thrust of America that he began... the ideas and the ideals, which he so nobly represented, must—and will—be translated into effective action."[6]

The son of a Texas legislator, Lyndon Johnson was born to be a politician. As a youth, he eagerly accompanied his father to the legislature and on his campaign trails. As he grew older, Johnson exhibited a natural propensity and unmatched enthusiasm for the field of politics. Years spent participating in student government and debate teams as a young man helped prepare Johnson for a life in public office.

Johnson was a talker, but also a listener, and he possessed a natural ability to read others. He understood the importance and power of relationships, and used that understanding to his advantage throughout his life. Perceptive to what made people tick, Johnson was able to appeal to individual interests when pitching his legislation, employing something his Washington colleagues came to know as "the Johnson treatment." Standing at six feet four inches tall, Johnson would use his imposing height and physical presence to both intimidate and awe, leaning in close to pressure or cajole in his pursuit of agreement or compromise. Johnson could be either domineering and harsh or warm and understanding, and he inspired both resentment and devotion in those around him. He quickly gained a reputation for being shrewd and opportunistic, but also brilliant and effective.

Johnson's ability to effectively work with Congress was a major advantage to him as president. He used the influence and expertise he had gained while on the Senate floor to push major legislation through that otherwise might have languished in Congress indefinitely. In regard to his relations with Congress and ability to achieve new legislation, historians rank Lyndon Johnson as one of the very best among U.S. Presidents, falling just bellow the bar set by America's longest-serving president, Franklin D. Roosevelt.[7]

Johnson used his influence to ask difficult favors of key lawmakers, and when they came through for him, he never took it for granted. One such time was when the Civil Rights Bill of 1964 resulted in the longest filibuster in Senate history, with fifty-seven days of debate waged over a seventy-three-day period. When the filibuster finally ended and voting commenced, the bill passed, but with only six southern votes in its favor. After the bill passed, one of the southern congressmen who had voted in favor of the controversial legislation received a late-night phone call from President Johnson, who said, "The reason I am calling is I want you to know that your president is extremely proud of you... I didn't want this night to go by until I called on you personally to tell you how proud I am of you."[8]

~၁•၇~

FAIR-MINDED – desiring and pursuing equal justice for all; fair, impartial, unprejudiced, empathetic, understanding.

Great leadership is marked by sincere concern for the welfare and betterment of people. Leadership is largely ineffective if its focus is self-serving and it fails to benefit those it affects. Fair-minded leaders see the value and potential in every individual whom they lead, regardless of differences, and they use their power and influence to improve every person's wellbeing and to bring justice for all.

L yndon B. Johnson was one of the most active U.S. Presidents of all time in regard to civil rights and social equality, and is considered by historians to rank just under Abraham Lincoln in his pursuit of equal justice for all.[9] Johnson's dream and true passion was the building of the Great Society. He used his position as president to force the government to confront the needs of the nation like never before—particularly in regards to poverty and racial discrimination.

Early in his presidency Johnson declared "War on Poverty," saying, "I don't know whether I will pass a single law, or get a single dollar appropriated, but before I'm through, no community in America is going to be able to ignore the poverty in its midst."[10] He went on to prepare and pass bill after bill, signing into law funds and programs designed to help "free thirty million Americans from the prison of poverty."[11] Johnson energetically pursued his vision of helping the disadvantaged to help themselves, believing those caught in poverty just needed a helping hand to lift them up so that they could make their own way. He condemned discrimination and championed better education and job training for the poor and minorities.

In addition to the War on Poverty, Johnson actively pursued the rest of his Great Society agenda, passing bills for education, conservation, consumer protection, urban renewal, public housing, national humanities and arts, and much more. Most notably, he boldly addressed the growing unrest known as the civil rights movement. Johnson swiftly embraced the civil rights bill that Kennedy had proposed just months before his death, and successfully pushed it through Congress just seven months after becoming president. The next year, he proposed and soon signed into law the Voting Rights Act of 1965.

President Johnson passionately wanted to address each and every one of the nation's problems and find ways to fix everything. He wanted to do great things on the domestic front and improve the lives of Americans across the nation. But sadly, the quagmire of the Vietnam War demanded much of Johnson's attention and energies, and effectively sucked the life and credibility out of his administration.

The Vietnam War was a dilemma Johnson never wanted to be involved in, but did not know how to avoid. Stuck between a rock and a hard place, Johnson had to make the painful decision to either give in to the communist aggressors and withdraw from South Vietnam, or to press on, hoping to stop the advance of communism. He relied heavily on the counsel of men whom he felt were better educated and equipped to analyze the growing conflict. Ultimately, his decision to escalate American involvement in the unpopular war was Johnson's downfall, tarnishing his reputation and casting a shadow over his many valuable contributions and accomplishments.

With the weight of the war and the deaths of thousands of American soldiers on his shoulders, Johnson chose not to run for reelection in 1968. Upon the inauguration of President Richard Nixon on January 20, 1969, Lyndon Johnson retired with his wife, Lady Bird, to their ranch in central Texas. He died four years later, just one day before the Paris Peace Accords signaled the end of direct U.S. involvement in Vietnam. While his legacy is clouded by the war, President Lyndon Baines Johnson accomplished many great things for his beloved nation, marking his place in American history as one of triumph as well as tragedy.

~⌒⌒~

7

RICHARD NIXON
PRESIDENTIAL LIBRARY & MUSEUM
Yorba Linda, California

I was pleasantly surprised by my visit to the Richard Nixon Presidential Library and Museum, located in Yorba Linda, California, a suburb of L.A. Situated in the midst of private residences and small businesses, the modest nine-acre plot of land boasts beautiful landscaping and simple yet impressive buildings.

After stretching my legs in the parking lot and taking in the large fountain in front of the building, I walked in the front entrance where I was greeted by a life-size cardboard cutout of President Nixon and Elvis Presley shaking hands. After studying the lobby area and before beginning my tour of the museum's indoor exhibits, I stepped out into the courtyard to admire the beautiful reflecting pool and the colorful gardens—in full bloom on that warm April day. Palm trees, orange trees, and dozens of other vibrant trees and flowering shrubs line the courtyard and surround the long, shallow pool. Buildings hem in the courtyard on three sides, and the fourth is bordered by

Reflecting pool and courtyard outside the library and museum

the gently sloping Pat Nixon Outdoor Amphitheater. Beyond the amphitheater I could see the thirty-seventh president's birthplace and childhood home, but I chose to first explore the indoor exhibits before venturing further.

Back inside, I began slowly walking through the displays, experiencing up close a unique piece of American history. I was intrigued by the expansive campaign gallery, the displays detailing Nixon's busy vice presidency and presidency, and a room full of bronze statues depicting the likenesses of ten renowned world leaders, including Soviet leader Nikita Khrushchev, Israel's Golda Meir, France's Charles de Gaulle, and Britain's Winston Churchill. I found the Watergate exhibit to be fascinating and remarkably comprehensive, candidly laying bare the unsavory details of the Nixon administration's indiscretions and national disgrace. The exhibit appears to hold back nothing, sharing the unpleasant truths with visitors, and maybe most importantly, reminding us that even United States Presidents are only human.

After leaving the main museum galleries, I walked down a long stately hallway flanked with flags representing every state in America. At the end of the hallway I found myself in an exact replica of the White House East Room, complete with crystal chandeliers and a

Replica of the White House East Room

large reproduction of the George Washington portrait. After admiring the unique event hall, it was time to check out Nixon's birthplace and childhood home. When I set foot inside the modest two-story farmhouse built by Richard Nixon's father, Frank, I truly felt like I'd been transported back in time. Here was the highchair the future president sat in as an infant, and there was the original Crown piano that he learned to play as a little boy. There were yellowing *National Geographic* magazines from 1920 sitting on an end table, and a beautiful black and silver St. Clair wood stove from Belleville Stove Works in the kitchen.

When I finished admiring the historical little house with its antique furnishings, I stepped back outside and walked over to the gravesite of the former President and First Lady. I paid my respects in front of their simple headstones before quietly moving on to check out the Army One helicopter that Nixon used while president, and then back inside the museum to make sure I hadn't missed anything. My last stop was an exhibit called "A Trip Back in *TIME*," a display of fifty-four *TIME* magazine covers all featuring Richard Nixon. To date, Nixon has appeared on the cover of *TIME* magazine more than any other person in history. His first appearance on the cover was in 1952, when he was nominated for vice president, and his last

**Portraits of Richard and Pat Nixon on display in the
museum's temporary exhibit gallery**

appearance was the week of his death, in April 1994.

When I first set out to visit the Richard Nixon Presidential Library and Museum, I really did not know what to expect. But when I arrived and began my tour, I was pleasantly surprised and impressed with the library and museum, describing it in my own mind as "understated with class." As I finished my visit at the end of the day and drove away, I marveled at the extraordinary life, career and accomplishments of this one man. Richard Nixon served his country as a U.S. congressman, senator, vice president, president, and as an influential elder statesman. While his legacy is mixed, one cannot deny that his life was marked by remarkable achievements and victory over incredible odds. Born in the farmhouse his father built, Nixon lived a full and eventful life before being buried behind that same house eighty-one years later.

～〇〇〇～

Hallway lined with flags from each state in America

**Display featuring memorabilia and photographs from
Nixon's first bid for the presidency**

Did You Know?

Richard Nixon and three of his four brothers were named after legendary kings of England—Richard was named after King Richard the Lionheart.

Large presidential seal on floor of museum foyer

Sculptures within the World Leaders Gallery

Did You Know?

In 1938 Nixon cofounded and became president of a company called Citra-Frost that attempted to freeze and sell orange juice. The venture ultimately failed, and Nixon left the citrus business for good.

A portion of the exhibit depicting the details and drama of Watergate

Exhibit of fifty-four *TIME* magazine covers all featuring Richard Nixon

Did You Know?

Richard Nixon is one of only two people in U.S. history to have been on a major political party's presidential ticket five times— the other is Franklin D. Roosevelt.

View of courtyard and Pat Nixon outdoor amphitheater

Richard Nixon's birthplace and boyhood home

Did You Know?
Richard Nixon was the first U.S. President to visit all fifty states and also the first to visit China.

The piano Nixon played as a boy, inside his boyhood home

Army One helicopter that carried Nixon during his presidency

Did You Know?

On January 20, 1969, Richard Nixon spoke with American astronauts on the moon by radiotelephone. This historic phone call is known as the longest distance telephone call ever made.

Gravesite of Richard and Pat Nixon

WHEN YOU VISIT...
DON'T MISS THESE:

- Beautiful courtyard and reflecting pool
- Richard Nixon's birthplace cottage
- Pat Nixon amphitheater
- Army One helicopter
- Gravesite of Richard and Pat Nixon
- Replica of White House East Room
- World Leaders gallery
- Original manuscript of "God Bless America" by Irving Berlin
- Nixon's presidential limousine
- Watergate exhibit
- Hallway lined with state flags
- "A Trip Back in *TIME*" exhibit

To see many more photos—in full color—please visit
www.presidentialleadershipbook.com/richard-nixon/photos

"Only if you have been in the deepest valley, can you ever know how magnificent it is to be on the highest mountain."

"If you take no risks, you will suffer no defeats. But if you take no risks, you win no victories."

"We must always remember that America is a great nation today not because of what government did for people but because of what people did for themselves and for one another."

RICHARD NIXON
Ambitious, Resolved, and *Persevering*

FULL NAME: Richard Milhous Nixon
LIFESPAN: 81 years (1913 – 1994)
TERM: 37th President (R) 1969 – 1974

Richard Nixon remains one of the most polarizing presidents in American history, best remembered not for the
accomplishments of his presidency, but for the scandal that ended
it. Nonetheless, if the time is taken to look beyond the national disgrace of Watergate, one can see that Nixon exhibited several valuable
traits that helped him in his remarkable climb to the nation's highest
position of leadership.

AMBITIOUS - eager to obtain or achieve a specific goal, such as success, power, fame, or wealth; strongly desirous, eager, aspiring, enterprising.

Ambitious leaders possess an earnest desire for achievement or distinction. Their ambition propels them forward, tirelessly endeavoring for the fulfillment of that desire. When others may slack or give up, truly ambitious leaders keep going, their eyes unwaveringly fixed on the prize.

From his childhood and throughout his adult life and political career, Richard Nixon was an introverted and naturally reserved individual. However, from the time he was a boy, Nixon wanted to be somebody great. It was this ambition that enabled him to pursue a life in public office despite his introversion. As a youth Nixon poured himself into his studies and pursued activities like student government and debate club, which helped prepare him for his yet unseen future in politics.

Though his excellent grades could have taken him to an Ivy League school, family demands and financial constraints limited Nixon to a modest local college in Whittier, California. While at Whittier College, Nixon helped organize a men's club called the Orthogonians, which meant "sharp shooters." The society was made up of young men who took pride in working their way through college and striving to reach their full potential. Driven to excel wherever he was, Nixon's hard work while at Whittier College paid off, winning him a full scholarship to Duke University Law School.

After graduating from Duke, Nixon returned to California where he took a position with a small law firm in Whittier. Though the law firm wasn't large and prestigious like those Nixon originally had his eye on, he didn't let his humble start as a lawyer dampen his ambitions. Nixon began to develop political aspirations, and after the outbreak of World War II he took a government position in the Office of Price Administration (OPA)—the federal agency in charge of regulating wartime prices and overseeing rationing. This allowed Nixon to leave California and move to Washington, D.C. However, less than a year later, he chose to help the war effort in a more tangible way, leaving the OPA and entering the navy in August of 1942.

Though he saw no actual combat, Nixon received two service stars and several commendations during his naval career, which ended with the war in 1945. He was officially discharged as a lieutenant commander in March 1946, and quickly set out on the path toward public office once again. He soon found an opportunity to enter politics when a group of prominent Republicans from his home state of California approached him about running for the U.S. Congress that year. Nixon accepted the invitation, and soon was waging his first of many political campaigns.

Nixon's first campaign truly revealed his internal drive, focus, and fierce determination to succeed. Nixon was relentless, crafting a hard-hitting, mud-slinging campaign that set the pattern for his future campaigns and succeeded in winning him a seat in the House, where he remained until being elected to the Senate four years later. Though Nixon's denigrative campaigning strategies have been frowned upon, they serve to reveal the man's steel resolve to do whatever he saw as necessary to achieve his mission.

RESOLVED - set firmly in purpose, intent or belief; holding fast to a set course; possessing nerve and grit; determined, tenacious, tough, unyielding, resolute.

Leaders who are truly resolved in purpose can remain steadfast and undaunted even in the face of extreme adversity and opposition—something every leader will experience. Leaders with steel resolve don't let negative circumstances or critics sway them, and they demonstrate patience and composure in trying times.

Nixon faced challenge after challenge throughout his life and political career. His fierce drive not only propelled him to overcome and succeed, it served to fuel his confidence and determination. Unwilling to ever succumb to failure and reluctant to show weakness, Nixon refused to back down from challenges or confrontation. While ultimately his steel resolve may have hurt him more than helped him, it enabled him to see the toughest challenges through to the end, and to handle many crises with remarkable steadiness and composure.

During the early years of Nixon's political career, while serving in the House of Representatives, he took a major investigative role in the controversial case of Alger Hiss, a high-ranking U.S. official who had been accused of being a communist spy for the Soviet Union. This extremely high-profile case brought Nixon into the national spotlight—a delicate position that, depending on how he handled himself, could have severely damaged his reputation and political career as easily as strengthened it. Despite the political risk, Nixon remained resolute, and it was primarily because of his dogged persistence that Hiss was ultimately convicted. The widespread recognition Nixon received as a result of the case helped him propel his career forward and win election to the U.S. Senate soon after.

Another crisis that Nixon handled with steady nerve and cool resolve was the controversy of his supposed "slush fund" during his vice-presidential campaign in 1952. Ignoring detractors' demands that he remove himself from Eisenhower's ticket, Nixon boldly handled the precarious situation by directly addressing the rumors during a televised address to the nation. In what came to be known as his "Checkers Speech," Nixon dispelled public concern about the campaign fund by openly sharing all of his personal finances, explaining exactly what the fund in question was and how it was used. He declared that he had accepted no political favors—with the exception of one gift he intended to keep—a little dog that his six-year-old daughter had named Checkers. Thanks to his calm and candid handling of the incident, Nixon saved his candidacy and rode the Eisenhower ticket into the White House, where he served as vice president for eight years.

Nixon was one of the most active and visible vice presidents in American history. President Eisenhower relied upon his young vice president to do a variety of difficult political assignments, and no matter the difficulty, Nixon's steady determination to succeed allowed him to perform smoothly in whatever role the president asked of him. In 1955 President Eisenhower suffered a severe heart attack, which put him in the hospital for seven weeks. In his absence, Vice President Nixon performed admirably. Acting carefully so as not to step out of bounds in the delicate situation, Nixon observed proper protocol yet provided steady leadership, as he put it, "without appearing to lead."[1]

In addition to his understated but firm handling of affairs during the president's convalescence, Vice President Nixon again showed his ability to handle difficult and high-stress situations through several other incidents during his vice presidency. While visiting South America as a representative of the United States in 1958, Nixon's motorcade was violently attacked by angry anti-American protesters. His cool composure during the frightening ordeal strengthened his reputation as a man of courage and steady resolve. The next year, while representing the United States during a trip to the Soviet Union, Nixon engaged Soviet leader Nikita Khrushchev in an impromptu discussion that turned heated. This televised confrontation, famously known as "the Kitchen Debate," again left American viewers with a positive impression of Nixon's nerve and competence as their vice president.

PERSEVERING – resolutely persistent; maintaining a purpose despite difficulty, opposition, or discouragement; determined, focused, resilient, irrepressible.

Every leader will experience significant setbacks, mistakes and failures during their lifetime and career. The ability and determination to persevere despite these inevitable difficulties is a mark of strong leaders. Persevering leaders possess stamina and grit, able to overcome many hurdles, losses, or even public disgrace.

Arguably Nixon's most remarkable trait was his perseverance, resilience and ability to bounce back from adversity and setbacks. Even as a youth, not much came easy for Richard Nixon. His family's financial hardships limited his opportunities, though he was an exceptional student who showed great potential. Even when forced to turn down a scholarship to Harvard because he couldn't afford the travel or living expenses, Nixon persevered, making the best of his circumstances. Proving himself at a more affordable local college, Nixon overcame his disadvantage and changed his fortunes, wining a full ride to law school.

Following a brief career as a lawyer, a few months with the OPA, and three years in the navy during World War II, Nixon found the primary career that he would pursue for the rest of his life—that of a politician and public figure. Nixon enjoyed many successes as a politician, but he also experienced significant setbacks. In the 1960 presidential election, Nixon lost to the charismatic Democratic candidate, John F. Kennedy, by just 0.2 percent of the popular vote—the narrowest margin of the twentieth century. Nixon returned to California in defeat, but he was not finished; as Nixon once said, "A man is not finished when he is defeated. He is finished when he quits."[2]

Nixon was not a quitter. Less than two years later, he ran in the California gubernatorial race against incumbent Edmund G. "Pat" Brown. However, after just being a hairsbreadth away from the presidency, Nixon's heart wasn't set on becoming governor, and without his trademark focus and determination at the helm of his campaign, he suffered another stinging defeat at the polls, this time by a much wider margin. Disappointed by the loss and angered by how he had been portrayed by the media, Nixon declared to members of the press after the election, "You don't have Nixon to kick around anymore, because, gentlemen, this is my last press conference!"[3] But even after that seemingly final word, Nixon just didn't have it in him to give up. He returned to private life again as a lawyer, but over the next six years he quietly prepared for another run for the presidency. In 1968, Nixon's dogged perseverance and determination paid off, and after another infamous campaign, he was elected as the thirty-seventh President of the United States.

By far the greatest show of Nixon's resilience and fortitude came toward the end of his life, following his resignation from the presidency. When a disgraced Nixon left the White House in 1974, his life was in shambles. Ambitious to a fault, he had made a series of dishonorable choices in his quest for power that ultimately led to the infamous Watergate scandal and his downfall. In addition to his national disgrace, Nixon faced financial troubles and physical ailments, ending the year at one of the lowest points in his life. But if there was one thing that Nixon did extremely well, it was rebound from adversity.

Over the next twenty years, Nixon slowly rebuilt his life, authoring several well-regarded books, giving speeches, and offering his expertise on foreign policy. Through pure determination and perseverance, Nixon made a remarkable comeback during his post-presidency years, slowly becoming known by world and national leaders as a respected elder statesman. Nixon died in 1994, and while he left behind a mixed legacy, his is ultimately a story of survival—a tale of triumph over defeat. As Nixon wisely noted, "You've got to learn to survive a defeat. That's when you develop character."[4]

8

GERALD R. FORD
PRESIDENTIAL LIBRARY & MUSEUM
Ann Arbor and Grand Rapids, Michigan

Unlike the other presidential libraries and museums, which typically house the archives and historical materials together with or next door to the museum exhibits, the Gerald Ford Presidential Library and Presidential Museum are two distinct facilities located in separate cities. However, even with the separation, they are considered to be a single institution and share one director.

My most recent visit to the Gerald Ford Presidential Museum in Grand Rapids, Michigan was in late spring. The weather was perfect, with clear blue skies and an inviting breeze that caused the trees and the American flag out front to gently wave in greeting. Located downtown on the banks of the Grand River, the glass front of the sleek two-story triangular building displays a shimmering reflection of the Grand Rapids skyline. Just in front of the doors, a bronze sculpture of President Ford greets museum visitors as they pass by.

I breathed in the fresh air, enjoying the view over the river and

Bronze sculpture of Gerald Ford located in front of the museum

admiring the long shallow pool stretched in front of the building, with a bubbling fountain at one end. After taking in the view, I strolled past a colorful garden honoring the late Betty Ford, which lies between the pool and the shining wall of windows. Just beyond the museum I came to an ornate metal fence that encloses the gravesite of the former President and First Lady. As I entered the burial site, I was impressed by the quiet beauty of the place; large graceful trees shade the curved alcove and lend their stately elegance to the peaceful atmosphere. The gravesite is flanked by stone planters overflowing with flowers, and through the trees the afternoon sunlight casts dappled shadows over the graves. The landscaping is simple yet beautiful, and it is apparent that loving care is taken in its upkeep.

After pausing to reflect for a few minutes, I made my way back to the entrance of the building and went inside to begin my tour. The large, open lobby area is home to several displays, including a portion of the Berlin Wall and a life-size sculpture depicting Ford as a fourteen-year-old Eagle Scout. Once inside the galleries, I explored the replica Oval Office as it appeared during Ford's administration, then moved on to reminisce over 1970s pop culture memorabilia. After that it was on to learn more about Ford's early life and congressional

Eagle sculpture set within the Betty Ford Garden *(museum)*

career before taking in the exhibits representing his presidential leadership and diplomacy. I learned many new details of Ford's life and presidency, and was reminded of things I had forgotten, like his two close calls with would-be assassins in September 1975, and that he presided over the United States' bicentennial celebration in July 1976.

By the time I emerged from the museum several hours after my arrival, I had a much greater understanding and respect for the life and legacy of the thirty-eighth U.S. President. I decided to take a few minutes to revisit his final resting place, where I spent some time reflecting on the things I'd seen, heard, and experienced that day.

My visit to the Gerald R. Ford Presidential Library, on the campus of the University of Michigan in Ann Arbor, was much shorter than my tour of the museum. The library's main purpose is to collect, preserve, and make accessible to researchers archival materials relating to the life and presidency of Gerald Ford. The library also serves as a repository and research facility for materials relating to U.S. affairs during the Cold War era. Since I wasn't there as a registered researcher, I did not delve into the archives. Instead, I remained in the lobby area, which is home to a number of interesting displays—unique from the exhibits I saw at the museum.

Here I enjoyed learning much more about First Lady Betty Ford,

The Gerald R. Ford Presidential Library in Ann Arbor, MI

from her childhood through her dancing career to her marriage and finally to her life as a politician's wife and public figure. I also learned much more about Gerald Ford's college days and promising football talent that I hadn't known before—here was where I first learned that Ford had received offers of professional football contracts from both the Detroit Lions and the Green Bay Packers! He declined, choosing instead to get a law degree from Yale Law School.

After perusing the exhibits in the spacious two-story lobby, I stepped out back into a small outdoor plaza. Just on the edge of the lawn, hidden in the shadows of the trees, I caught a glimpse of a deer that no doubt was enjoying the well-watered grass. I then turned my attention to the focal point of the brick patio, a large stainless steel kinetic sculpture that entrances viewers with its hypnotic movement. After enjoying the spring sunshine for a few minutes, I went back inside to take some more photos and finish my tour. As I left the library and walked back to the parking lot, I couldn't help but marvel at how much incredible information must be stored in that modest brick building. I certainly had learned a lot that I hadn't known several hours before, and I hadn't even scratched the surface of what's contained in the library's archives!

Various exhibits within the lobby of Ford's presidential library

Exhibit at the library depicting Ford's college football days

Did You Know?

Gerald R. Ford was born Leslie Lynch King, Jr., named after his biological father, but his parents separated only a few weeks after his birth. Two and a half years later his mother remarried, and he became known as Gerald R. Ford, Jr. after his stepfather. He legally changed his name when he was twenty-two.

Sculpture of young Gerald Ford as an Eagle Scout *(museum)*

Exhibits featuring Ford's naval service during World War II *(museum)*

Did You Know?

As part of his efforts to work his way through law school, Gerald Ford served as a seasonal park ranger at Yellowstone National Park in the summer of 1936. He also worked briefly as a fashion model in the early 1940s, appearing in Cosmopolitan and Look magazines.

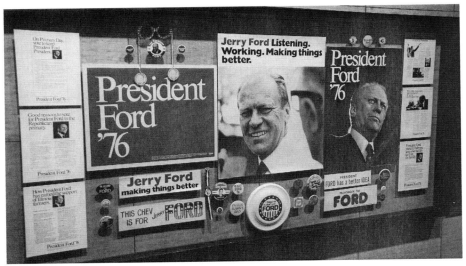

**Display featuring posters and memorabilia from
Ford's presidential campaign** *(museum)*

Replica of President Ford's Oval Office *(museum)*

Did You Know?

President Ford survived two separate assassination attempts unscathed. Though apparently unrelated, both assassination attempts were made by women, and both occurred in the state of California in September, 1975, just seventeen days apart.

Replica of President Ford's Cabinet Room *(museum)*

Display showing memorabilia from America's bicentennial celebration in 1976 *(museum)*

Did You Know?

President Ford's wife, First Lady Betty Ford, danced on the Cabinet Room table the day before the Fords left the White House.

Scenic area outside of the Fords' gravesite *(museum)*

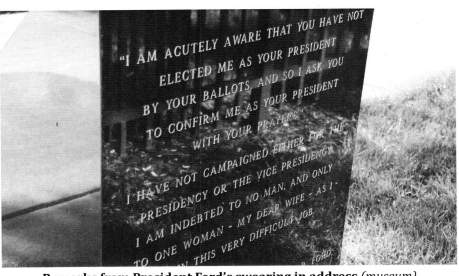

"I AM ACUTELY AWARE THAT YOU HAVE NOT ELECTED ME AS YOUR PRESIDENT BY YOUR BALLOTS, AND SO I ASK YOU TO CONFIRM ME AS YOUR PRESIDENT WITH YOUR PRAYERS." I HAVE NOT CAMPAIGNED EITHER FOR THE PRESIDENCY OR THE VICE PRESIDENCY. I AM INDEBTED TO NO MAN, AND ONLY TO ONE WOMAN - MY DEAR WIFE - AS I ... IN THIS VERY DIFFICULT JOB. FORD

Remarks from President Ford's swearing in address *(museum)*

Did You Know?

Ford did not spend his first night as president at the White House. Like they'd done so many nights before, the Ford family cooked dinner and spent the night at their modest brick home just outside of Washington.

Gravesite of Gerald and Betty Ford *(museum)*

WHEN YOU VISIT...
DON'T MISS THESE:

- Beautiful grounds of the presidential museum
- Betty Ford Garden
- Gravesite of Gerald and Betty Ford
- Young Jerry Ford gallery and "Growing up Grand" exhibits
- Exhibits depicting Ford's college and football days
- Gallery featuring memorabilia and news stories of the 1970s
- Watergate exhibit
- Display of White House switchboard
- Replicas of Ford's Oval Office and Cabinet Room
- Exhibits featuring America's bicentennial celebration
- The Ford Presidential Library and exhibits in Ann Arbor

To see many more photos—in full color—please visit
www.presidentialleadershipbook.com/gerald-ford/photos

"The ultimate test of leadership is not the polls you take, but the risks you take... the greatest defeat of all would be to live without courage, for that would hardly be living at all."

"A nation survives only so long as the spirit of sacrifice and self-discipline is strong within its people."

"History and experience tell us that moral progress comes not in comfortable and complacent times, but out of trial and confusion."

GERALD FORD
Amiable, Strong in Character, and *Candid*

FULL NAME: Gerald Rudolph Ford
LIFESPAN: 93 years (1913 – 2006)
TERM: 38th President (R) 1974 – 1977

Though it lasted less than two and a half years, the presidency of President Gerald R. Ford marked a significant period in American history and will not soon be forgotten. The only U.S. President to have not sought nor been elected to that office, "Jerry" Ford became president in the midst of chaos and national scandal. Among his memorable first words to the American people upon taking the oath of the presidency were, "My fellow Americans, our long national nightmare is over."[1] The presidency of Gerald R. Ford promised to reestablish dignity and decency in the White House and to restore a nation's faith in its highest elected leader.

153

AMIABLE – having a pleasant, gracious, and good-natured personality; acting genuinely and without pretension; connecting with others; friendly, sociable, affable, agreeable.

Likeability may not be a leadership requirement, but it certainly is a very valuable leadership asset. Amiable leaders are well liked due to their genuine and gracious demeanor. Their ability to connect with others and build relationships gives them a clear advantage over leaders who are unpleasant and rude or distant and aloof.

Ford was a popular and athletic student; he excelled in academics as well as sports, and as a high school senior he caught the attention of the University of Michigan. Though he was a star football player, at that time no football scholarships existed at the University of Michigan, and Ford's family couldn't afford the tuition of fifty dollars per semester. However, the young, well-liked Jerry Ford had earned the respect of his high school principal, Arthur Krause, who privately decided to help the boy go to college. With a few phone calls and some string-pulling, Krause came up with a scholarship to cover Ford's tuition, and he enrolled at the University of Michigan in 1931.

Ford continued his top-performance as a college football player, earning recognition as a team player and natural leader, and was voted most valuable player during his senior year. Popular and sociable both on and off the field, Ford was a model student and athlete. He had the opportunity to play professional football after college, but instead chose to pursue a law degree at Yale University. His athletic skill continued to help him even at Yale, where he took a job as the boxing coach and assistant varsity football coach. Initially the administration at Yale was reluctant to admit Ford to the law program because of his demanding coaching duties, but they relented in 1938. Ford proved himself as both an excellent coach and as a capable law student, going on to graduate in the top third of his class in 1941.

Similar to his predecessor, Richard Nixon, young Ford spent a short while practicing law after passing the bar exam, then enlisted in the navy after the United States entered World War II. Ford served for four years, both stateside and aboard the USS *Monterey* in the South Pacific, before being honorably discharged in 1946 as a lieutenant commander. After leaving the navy, Ford returned to Michigan and to practicing law, where his interest in politics began to grow. In 1948 he ran for U.S. Congress and won a seat in the House, effectively launching his political career. The young, friendly Michigan politician soon earned the respect and admiration of his constituents, who reelected him for twelve more consecutive terms, each time giving him more than sixty percent of the vote.

Congressman Ford earned a reputation of being genuine and easy-going. He might have had opponents on Capitol Hill, but never enemies. Ford was widely known for the unparalleled decency with which he treated everyone, and he forged many lasting friendships. Throughout his twenty-five years in Congress, Ford remained engaged and involved with the people in his district. An unpretentious man, he possessed a natural ability to connect to the common man, and his genuineness appealed to everyone.

Perhaps most notable of the traits Ford demonstrated in Congress was his ability to reach across party lines and work out compromises between Republicans and Democrats. As he had proven on the football field years earlier, he was a team player. Ford was pragmatic; though he had strong political convictions, he also recognized the value of flexibility and compromise as tools for progress. Ford's reputation for fairness and decency earned the respect of his fellow congressmen, and it was because members of both parties held him in such high-esteem that he was chosen and confirmed as the vice-presidential replacement when Spiro Agnew resigned in 1973. Little did Ford know that just eight months later he would again be called upon as a replacement—this time for President Richard Nixon.

⌐◠⸭◠⌐

STRONG IN CHARACTER - possessing strength of character; demonstrating qualities of honesty, courage, integrity, and steadfastness; moral, ethical, upright, resolved, purposeful.

Leaders with strength of character act out of conviction and with a solid sense of purpose. Demonstrating integrity and courage, they do what they think is right because it is right, not because it's easy or convenient. Principled and steadfast, leaders who possess strength of character are trustworthy and loyal even in the most trying circumstances.

Though he had been a successful politician for a quarter of a century, Gerald R. Ford never had his eyes set on the Oval Office. The highest political ambition of this humble, unassuming man from Michigan was to become the Speaker of the House—a goal he never reached, though he did serve as the House minority leader for eight years. Nonetheless, when the presidency was thrust upon him on August 9, 1974, Ford declared to a nation in turmoil, "I have not sought this enormous responsibility, but I will not shirk it."[2]

As he had acknowledged, the new president faced an enormous responsibility brought about by unprecedented circumstances. Due to the misconduct of the previous administration, the executive office was plagued by scandal and cloaked in disgrace. Ford faced a disillusioned and wary nation that had lost faith in its government. He inherited a desk in the Oval Office piled high with problems, including the notorious Watergate scandal, a beleaguered economy, diplomatic and international concerns, and military problems—most significantly the prolonged end of the Vietnam War. Though Ford had not had the same opportunity of the normal planning, preparation and transition months experienced by presidents who are elected, he remained true to his word, shirking none of these immense responsibilities and facing the chaos with fortitude.

As a first step toward moving beyond the Watergate scandal that the nation and his newly inherited administration were so deeply mired in, President Ford made the most controversial decision of his presidency just one month after being sworn in. On September

8, 1974, Ford offered a full presidential pardon to Richard Nixon for any crimes he may have committed as president. As a result of this announcement, Ford's approval ratings plummeted, and as now seen through the lens of history, irreparable damage was done to his chances of winning the 1976 election.

Ford knew his decision to pardon Nixon would be hugely unpopular. The national sentiment was anything but forgiving toward his predecessor who had so clearly abused his executive powers. Most of the American people wanted justice for Richard Nixon, not mercy. Despite the blow he knew he would take to his popularity and reputation, Ford felt that it was the right thing to do for the overall good of the nation. He saw nothing good coming from continued national focus on the Watergate fiasco and protracted criminal proceedings. Believing that too much of his time and focus were being spent dealing with the Watergate scandal in light of other national crises that needed his attention, Ford resolved to do what he felt was necessary to get Nixon's problems out of the White House and to lead the country forward.

Immediate results of the pardon included vehement criticism, public disparagement, and a twenty-two-point drop in Ford's approval ratings overnight. Despite the public rancor stirred up by his decision, and the widespread disapproval of his contemporaries, Ford maintained that it was the right thing to do and stayed the course under fire. It wasn't until decades later that historians and political pundits began to acknowledge the wisdom of Ford's controversial decision. In 2001 former President Ford was presented with the John F. Kennedy Profile in Courage Award for his actions regarding Watergate. As Senator Edward Kennedy presented the award, he explained:

> *At a time of national turmoil, America was fortunate that it was Gerald Ford who took the helm of the storm-tossed ship of state. Unlike many of us at the time, President Ford recognized that the nation had to move forward, and could not do so if there was a continuing effort to prosecute former President Nixon. So President Ford made a courageous decision... His courage and dedication to*

our country made it possible for us to begin the process of healing and put the tragedy of Watergate behind us.[3]

Just one week after announcing his pardon of Richard Nixon, Ford made another bold and controversial move, signing a proclamation that offered conditional amnesty to draft evaders and military deserters of the divisive Vietnam War. During the televised event, Ford explained that he was by no means condoning any treasonous deeds, but said, "Reconciliation calls for an act of mercy to bind the nation's wounds and to heal the scars of divisiveness."[4] Once again, Ford acted with conviction and courage, putting America's best interests above his own, and bravely facing the inevitable political fallout.

CANDID – acting and speaking openly and honestly; free from reservation, deception, or subterfuge; forthright, straightforward, truthful, sincere, trustworthy.

One of the most valuable assets leaders can have is the trust and respect of those whom they lead. Candid leaders are forthright and sincere, acting and speaking honestly and gradually earning the respect and loyalty of their followers. Conversely, leaders who prove to be untrustworthy or deceptive are unable to command respect and as a result are largely ineffective, particularly over the long run.

Though he made several controversial decisions and brought upon himself the ire of much of the nation, one thing Ford never did was break his inaugural promise to "follow my instincts of openness and candor with full confidence that honesty is always the best policy in the end."[5] In sharp contrast to his predecessor, President Ford demonstrated indisputable integrity. Ford considered trust to be the most essential ingredient in great leadership, and he certainly fostered trust in those he led.

Ford's habits of honesty and openness began in his youth. He credited his values to the influence of his family, whose rules of conduct included "Tell the truth, work hard, and come to dinner on time." He also attributed the development of his moral compass to the Boy Scouts, which he joined at the age of twelve, advancing to the rank of Eagle Scout just two years later. The important values he learned in his youth stuck with him throughout his political career, as expressed by one of his colleagues in Congress, Martha Griffiths: "In all the years I sat in the House, I never knew Mr. Ford to make a dishonest statement nor a statement part-true and part-false. He never attempted to shade a statement, and I never heard him utter an unkind word."[6]

President Ford's integrity and candor were appreciated internationally as well as in Washington, as he was able to forge important diplomatic relationships with foreign heads of state. Many of these connections became enduring friendships that he maintained even after leaving office in 1977.

Though his contemporaries initially dismissed him as the president who was never elected, history will remember Gerald R. Ford as the man who helped restore the confidence and pride of America during a time of national crisis. Decades after his administration had ended, President Ford's chief of staff, Dick Cheney, reflected on how Ford had shaped history, stating that after the Watergate scandal, Ford "was there when it ended to sort of bind up the nation's wounds, to restore people's confidence in government, and—simply by the sheer force of his character and his personal qualities—to restore trust and confidence, if you will, in the presidency and the White House. That was, I think, his single biggest contribution."[7] Thanks to the actions and humble, effective leadership of President Ford, when the nation celebrated its 200th birthday on July 4, 1976, it did so with great pride.

9

JIMMY CARTER
PRESIDENTIAL LIBRARY & MUSEUM
Atlanta, Georgia

The Jimmy Carter Presidential Library and Museum is adjacent to the Carter Center, a non-profit organization founded by Jimmy and Rosalynn Carter that works to advance human rights and alleviate human suffering across the world. Together these facilities form what is known as the Carter Presidential Center, which is located on a spacious thirty-five-acre park in Atlanta, Georgia.

One of the most prominent features of the Carter Presidential Center is the beautiful landscaping. From the rose garden in front of the museum to the natural oak forest on the southwest side of the park, the beauty of things that grow is on display in every direction. One of my first stops after I arrived at the center was the museum courtyard; the pool and fountains create a peaceful atmosphere perfect for unwinding after driving through Atlanta traffic. The courtyard opens to terraced flower gardens and an impressive circular display of the nation's state flags, with the American flag

The Carter Presidential Center Rose Garden

proudly flying in the middle.

After enjoying the peaceful outdoor setting for a few minutes, I headed inside to see what I could learn about the thirty-ninth President and First Lady. The first exhibits I came to detailed the early life of Jimmy Carter, including his childhood on the family peanut farm, his navy career, marriage to Rosalynn, and starting a family. I learned that he grew up during the Great Depression, that he wanted to join the navy from the time he was a little boy, and that he met his future wife of more than six decades while on leave from Annapolis.

As I proceeded through the various galleries, I learned much more about this man who started as a Georgia farm boy and grew up to become President of the United States and an international humanitarian. I also picked up some fun facts, like how the pilot of Air Force One during his administration was also named Jimmy Carter, or that President Carter received as a gift from Mexico a unique metamorphic portrait by renowned Mexican artist Octavio Ocampo. I noted a unique photo of Carter with three other U.S. Presidents—Richard Nixon, Gerald Ford and Ronald Reagan—and a later photo of Carter with four other U.S. Presidents—George H. W. Bush, Bill Clinton, George W. Bush and Barack Obama. How rare

Exhibits depicting Carter's early life and childhood

it is for the life of one U.S. President (after being elected) to overlap with the lives of so many others!

As I neared the end of my tour, I passed the exhibits that tell the story of the Carters' life after leaving the White House. I was impressed by the remarkable things they have accomplished in advancing human rights. Though he was disappointed not to win a second term in office, when Carter's presidency ended he started a new chapter in his life, a chapter that he feels is the best so far. Since he left office, Carter has received a number of awards honoring his humanitarian efforts, including the Nobel Peace Prize and, along with his wife, the Presidential Medal of Freedom.

When I stepped back outside after finishing my tour, I took a few minutes to enjoy the fresh air and to contemplate my visit. It was obvious that the Jimmy Carter Presidential Museum is relatively small in size compared to some of the other presidential museums, and also compared to the other buildings that make up the Carter Presidential Center, including the adjoining library. As I reflected on this, I realized that it's fitting. The man I learned about inside the museum is a simple, kind, and unpretentious man who has devoted his life—and his presidential center—to serving the world. It is apparent that he sees more value in a large archive of historical

Exhibits featuring Carter's service in the U.S. Navy submarine program

materials and a large center dedicated to advancing human rights than in a museum featuring his life and times. It is within these other facilities that Jimmy Carter's legacy can truly be found.

Did You Know?

Jimmy Carter is the longest surviving ex-president in U.S. History, surpassing the previous titleholder, Herbert Hoover, who lived 31 years, 231 days after leaving office.

Display featuring reproduction of the wedding ensemble worn by Jimmy and Rosalynn, and a photo of Jimmy in his Navy uniform

Exhibit depicting Carter's journey into public service

Did You Know?

To date, Jimmy Carter has authored twenty-seven books on a wide range of topics—from his childhood memories and personal poetry to U.S. politics and foreign relations, and even a children's book, "The Little Baby Snoogle-Fleejer," illustrated by his daughter, Amy.

I, JIMMY CARTER, DO SOLEMNLY SWEAR/
THAT I WILL FAITHFULLY EXECUTE/
THE OFFICE OF PRESIDENT OF THE
UNITED STATES/
AND WILL, TO THE BEST OF MY ABILITY/,
PRESERVE, PROTECT AND DEFEND/
THE CONSTITUTION OF THE UNITED STATES/
SO HELP ME GOD./

PRESENT—

Notecard used by the Chief Justice who administered Carter's oath of office

Displays featuring President Carter's inaugural celebration

Did You Know?

Jimmy Carter was the first president to be born in a hospital. The hospital where he was born is now the Lillian G. Carter Nursing Center, named after his mother who worked there as a registered nurse.

Exhibit depicting the Carters' continued efforts to advance human rights

Nobel Peace Prize awarded to Jimmy Carter in 2002

Did You Know?

During a speech in Japan, President Carter was delighted by the audience's laughter-filled response to one of his jokes. He later learned that the interpreter had not actually translated the joke, but instead had said, "President Carter told a funny story, everyone must laugh!"

View of courtyard and circle of flags outside the library and museum

WHEN YOU VISIT...
DON'T MISS THESE:

- Beautiful gardens and grounds of the presidential center
- Courtyard and reflecting pool
- Exhibits depicting Carter's life on the family peanut farm
- Gallery featuring Carter's naval career
- Replica of President Carter's Oval Office
- Remarkable portrait of Carter by artist Octavio Ocampo
- Exhibits depicting the Carters' commitment to waging peace and advancing human rights across the world
- Presidential Medals of Freedom, Nobel Peace Prize and other awards recognizing the Carters' humanitarian pursuits

To see many more photos—in full color—please visit
www.presidentialleadershipbook.com/jimmy-carter/photos

"As my high school teacher, Miss Julia Coleman, used to say: 'We must adjust to changing times and still hold to unchanging principles.'"

"Unless both sides win, no agreement can be permanent."

"The experience of democracy is like the experience of life itself—always changing, infinite in its variety, sometimes turbulent and all the more valuable for having been tested by adversity."

JIMMY CARTER
Conscientious, Industrious, and *a Peacemaker*

FULL NAME: James Earl Carter, Jr.
LIFESPAN: 89+ years (1924 –)
TERM: 39th President (D) 1977 – 1981

The limelight of the United States presidency was not kind to Jimmy Carter. Though being a "Washington outsider" had helped him reach the Oval Office in the election of 1976, it did not help him in his 1980 bid to stay there. His critics dismissed him as inexperienced and ineffective, and voters didn't give him another chance to prove himself. Only through the lens of time can the difficult challenges President Carter faced during his four years in office be seen, and it's only by examining his presidency in context with the years since he left office that one can really appreciate Jimmy Carter's accomplishments.

CONSCIENTIOUS - controlled by inner sense of what one believes is right; governed by conscience; principled, moral, careful, faithful, devoted.

Acting out of personal conviction and principles, conscientious leaders are devoted to a moral standard. Their strong commitment to their inner moral compass enables conscientious leaders to remain steadfast and dependable in the midst of outside pressure and changing times.

Jimmy Carter grew up in the rural South on his family's peanut farm in Plains, Georgia. He experienced firsthand the tragedies of the Great Depression and the deep racial prejudice so prevalent in that time and place. Contrary to societal norms, young Carter learned the value of equality and fairness from the example of his parents, and his commitment to racial and social equality has remained one of his core values throughout his life. As an adult, Carter has led a life of faith, endeavoring to live conscientiously and do what he personally feels is right.

After completing high school and one year at Georgia Institute of Technology, young Jimmy Carter won admission to the Naval Academy at Annapolis in 1943. He married Rosalynn Smith the same year of his graduation, and went on to serve seven years as a talented young naval officer. Lieutenant Carter was intelligent, hardworking and ambitious, with a very promising career ahead of him as an officer in the navy's nuclear submarine program. However, in 1953, Carter's father passed away, leaving behind a widow with a failing peanut farm. Jimmy Carter made the difficult decision to abandon his naval career in an attempt to save the family farm and help support his grieving mother. The move back to Plains was a painful one for the Carter family, and it serves as just one example of Carter's commitment to the welfare of others above his own self-interests.

Initially life back on the farm was very difficult, but the Carters' faith and perseverance saw them through the hard years, and by the end of the 1950s the family business was once again prosperous. Meanwhile, Carter became increasingly involved in his church and community, becoming a deacon and Sunday school teacher and serving on various civic boards. In 1958 Carter's commitment to his values were tested when a newly formed segregationist group called the White Citizens Council pressured him to join their ranks. His refusal resulted in a boycott of his business by members of the Council, but Carter—the only white male in Plains who wasn't a member—remained resolute, and eventually the boycott fizzled out. This public demonstration of Carter's steadfast commitment to do what he felt was right, even in the face of extreme opposition, made a lasting impression on the community.

Beginning in 1962, Carter entered state politics, serving two terms on the Georgia State Senate, and then going on to win the state gubernatorial election in 1970. After a remarkably short time in politics, Carter successfully ran for president in 1976, narrowly defeating his Republican opponent, incumbent Gerald Ford. The new president set the tone for his administration during the inaugural festivities as being more simple and low-key than many of his predecessors. He surprised the crowds—and his secret service detail—by stepping out of the presidential limousine and walking hand in hand with his wife in the parade from the Capitol to the White House. As historian Marvin Kranz noted, "He wanted to show people that he wasn't an aristocrat and that this wasn't a coronation… He wanted people to know he was a plain old peanut farmer from Georgia."[1] At the inaugural gala that evening, the President and First Lady led the nation in an understated but lively celebration of American diversity that resounded with hope for the future.

Jimmy Carter was anything but a perfect president, but his presidency was marked by his desire to always pursue what he felt was right—even though his perception of 'right' was not always supported and was seldom easy. He faced many opponents and critics for decisions he made and actions he took while president, but everything Carter did, he did in the pursuit of peace and in accordance with his deeply held convictions and Christian beliefs. As Carter once explained, "You can't divorce religious belief and public service. I've never detected any conflict between God's will and my political duty. If you violate one, you violate the other." Though those who did not share his convictions scorned Carter's leadership, he earned ardent support from many Americans who perceived his sincerity and good intentions. Nonetheless, in part because of those convictions and his refusal to play political games or schmooze his constituents, Carter lost reelection to the charming and popular Ronald Reagan in 1979.

~⌒⌒~

INDUSTRIOUS - working energetically and devotedly; pursuing a worthy goal; diligent, hardworking, enterprising, ambitious.

Industrious leaders are go-getters. Energetic and ambitious, they are eager to pursue worthy goals. Naturally productive and innovative, industrious leaders are usually very effective at developing strategies to reach their goals and lead their people and organization to success.

From the time he was a boy, Jimmy Carter yearned to do something great. An avid reader, young Carter imagined great adventures outside of the small rural Georgia community where he grew up. Inspired by his uncle's stories of life in the navy, Carter made up his mind that he was going to be a sailor. Before he was even in high school, the determined youth had requested a catalog from the U.S. Naval Academy in Annapolis, Maryland. Competition for admission was stiff at Annapolis, so Carter fervently committed himself to his studies in hopes of being selected as a cadet. In 1942 his childhood dream came true when he won appointment to the academy, enrolling in the spring of 1943. He graduated in the top ten percent of his class a year after the end of World War II.

As a young naval officer, Jimmy Carter continued to demonstrate a strong work ethic and a passion for serving his country. He selected the submarine service—one of the navy's most dangerous areas of duty—and his commitment and aptitude for the work impressed his commanding officers. In 1952 he was accepted into the new nuclear submarine program, and Lieutenant Carter was soon teaching nuclear engineering to submariners.

When Carter left the navy after his father's death in 1953, life changed dramatically for the young family. Leaving behind the exciting life of the navy was extremely difficult, but Carter put the same effort into farming as he had his promising naval career. Though times were hard, Carter poured himself into his work, and through sweat equity and effective management he was able to turn the farm into a profitable and successful business.

Farming in Plains, Georgia was a far shot from teaching nuclear engineering in Schenectady, New York, but Carter's new life offered a different set of adventures and opportunities. When not busy on the farm, Carter was busy in the community, joining a number of civic boards and becoming deeply involved in church. He experienced his first taste of public office when he ran successfully for a seat on the Sumter County Board of Education, and eventually became the chairman. Carter initially lost his first bid for the state senate in 1962, but he decided to ask for a recount, which revealed voter fraud that favored his opponent, and Carter was given another chance in a second election, which he won. He served two terms on the state senate before campaigning for the Democratic nomination for governor in 1966. Defeated in the primary, Carter was bitterly disappointed, but he immediately resolved to try again. Throughout his life, Carter has refused to fear failure: "My feeling is that if we refuse to try something that might fail, we lack faith either in ourselves or in our causes and goals."[2] A determined Jimmy Carter went on to win the next gubernatorial election, becoming the seventy-sixth governor of Georgia.

When Carter became president in 1977, he was truly a "Washington outsider." Unlike many of his predecessors, he arrived at the White House with no previous experience in national politics, and relatively few years of state politics under his belt. His unlikely yet rapid ascension to the presidency attested to the degree of ambition and determination Carter possessed. Carter carried that ambition into the Oval Office, where he hoped to use his power to help champion human rights, bring peaceful resolutions to international conflicts, and put measures in place to conserve energy and protect the environment.

While the proposals and policies of the Carter administration met with only modest success, Carter never stopped trying. Even when his presidency ended after his unsuccessful bid for reelection, Carter remained resolved to make his mark on the world in a positive way, much like one of his historical predecessors, former president Herbert Hoover. Jimmy Carter and his wife, Rosalynn, founded the Carter Center in 1982 to help carry out their vision of changing the world. The former president explains, "Ultimately, the work of The Carter Center is about helping people achieve better opportunities and watching hope take root where it languished before."[3] Through the center, Carter has continued to champion human rights and democracy, bring aid to the needy, and help mediate peace between conflicting governments. While it would have been easy to simply retire to Plains and quietly write his memoirs, Carter had no patience for retirement, choosing instead to use his golden years to help make a difference in the world.

PEACEMAKER - trying to establish peace; striving to reconcile parties that disagree or fight; empathetic, compassionate, altruistic.

Peacemakers recognize the innate value of every person and are perceptive to individual needs and perspectives. Because of their concern for people, peacemakers strive to use their talents to establish agreement or compromise whenever possible. Leaders who are peacemakers usually excel in conflict management and resolution, helping to prevent or to heal rifts between people and organizations.

Jimmy Carter is a peacemaker at heart. However, he is not necessarily a people pleaser. He once said, "If you fear making anyone mad, then you ultimately probe for the lowest common denominator of human achievement." Carter has long believed in peaceful resolutions, but he is not passive or weak-kneed, and he is not afraid to say or do what he feels needs to be said or done, no matter whose toes he steps on.

Balancing his desire for peace with his personal convictions and principles, President Carter was able to serve as a skillful mediator during the thirteen-day-long negotiations in 1979 between Egyptian president, Anwar El Sadat, and Israeli prime minister, Menachem Begin. In what came to be known as the Camp David Accords, President Carter relentlessly pursued peace between the two nations. His efforts have been widely credited with the ultimate result of a peace treaty that ended thirty years of conflict between Egypt and Israel.

To this day Carter remains very committed to peace worldwide and speaks out against military conflict except as a last resort, believing, as he once said, that "there should be an honest attempt at the reconciliation of differences before resorting to combat." Through the Carter Center, he has engaged in conflict resolution in more than a dozen countries since leaving the White House, and continues to be very involved in the promotion of democracy, human rights, and advances in health and agriculture in developing countries. In addition to their work with the Carter Center, Jimmy and Rosalynn Carter both regularly volunteer with Habitat for Humanity, a non-profit organization that helps provide homes for the needy around the world.

In 2002, Carter received the Nobel Peace Prize in recognition of his "decades of untiring effort to find peaceful solutions to international conflicts, to advance democracy and human rights, and to promote economic and social development."[4] While his presidency may not have gone down in history as being truly remarkable, Jimmy Carter's humanitarian and peacemaking efforts in the years since he left office have made an enduring mark on the world. He may not be remembered as one of the greatest American presidents, but Jimmy Carter certainly is leaving an admirable legacy as a leader who has positively impacted the world.

10

RONALD REAGAN
PRESIDENTIAL LIBRARY & MUSEUM
Simi Valley, California

I distinctly remember my first visit to the Ronald Reagan Presidential Library and Museum in Simi Valley, California. As I turned off of Madera Road and onto Presidential Drive, I could already tell I was in for a memorable experience. The long driveway, winding up the side of the hill, is lined with light posts, each with a banner bearing pictures and words related to American history or national monuments. As the road approaches the hill's summit, the banners begin to feature portraits of each U.S. President, from George Washington to Barack Obama.

When I rounded the corner at the top of the hill, I could at last see the library and museum, framed by a breathtaking view of the surrounding valley. Though I was eager to see the expansive and interactive exhibits I knew were inside, I couldn't help but spend my first hour outside, admiring the beautiful landscaping and panoramic views. I strolled across the grounds, enjoying the bright spring

A portion of the excellent panoramic view overlooking Simi Valley

sunshine and fresh air while I took photos. I stood for a moment to watch the flags in front of the museum slow dancing with the light breeze, and then I enjoyed a seat on one of the many benches overlooking the rolling hills of southern California. I was truly amazed at the beauty surrounding me, and I understood better than ever the allure of Reagan's California getaway, Rancho del Cielo, in the nearby Santa Ynez Mountains.

I made my way around to the other side of the building, where I found a replica White House South Lawn overlooking yet another stunning vista. After admiring the beautiful landscaping for a moment, I stepped over to the brightly painted section of the Berlin Wall. As I looked at that wall, once a symbol of oppression and now a monument to freedom, I could hear President Reagan's voice resonating in my head: "Mr. Gorbachev, tear down this wall!"[1]

Still musing over the worldwide impact of Ronald Reagan's life and presidency, I made my way to his final resting place to pay my respects. Vibrant plants and bright flowers surround the gently curved alcove, and a young orchard called "Gipper's Grove," planted in Reagan's honor, lies just to the south. On a clear day, if you turn to face the west while standing in front of his gravesite, you can just catch a glimpse of the Pacific Ocean beyond the hills. Though he was

"AMERICA'S BEST DAYS ARE YET TO COME. OUR PROUDEST MOMENTS ARE YET TO BE. OUR MOST GLORIOUS ACHIEVEMENTS ARE JUST AHEAD."

RONALD REAGAN

Bronze sculptures of the Reagans at the entrance to the museum galleries

raised in Illinois, the state of California became the home Reagan loved, and it was to this home he returned to ride into the sunset of his life. What a truly beautiful place to preserve the enduring legacy of the fortieth President of the United States.

When I finally stepped out of the April sunshine and into the museum to begin my tour, I found the exhibits to be just as captivating as the panoramic scenery outside. The very first display I came to was a life-size bronze sculpture of the fortieth President and First Lady, their smiles warmly welcoming visitors to the museum. Above the sculpture is a quote from the Great Communicator himself: "America's best days are yet to come. Our proudest moments are yet to be. Our most glorious achievements are just ahead."[2] It is this air of hope and anticipation that fills each gallery, leaving visitors not only with a better understanding of Ronald and Nancy Reagan's impact on the world, but also leaving them with a sense of wonder and inspiration.

Without a doubt, one of the most spectacular exhibits in the museum is the Air Force One Pavilion. As I walked down the long hallway approaching the giant airplane hangar, I simply wasn't prepared for what I was about to see. The nose of the plane came into view through the doorway, and then suddenly there it was—the

Air Force One, located inside a large three-story exhibit hangar

actual Air Force One aircraft that carried seven U.S. Presidents, from Richard Nixon to George W. Bush. With a wingspan of 145 feet 9 inches and a length of 152 feet 11 inches, the giant Boeing 707 is an impressive and imposing figure inside the large exhibit hangar that overlooks the valley. Facing a massive glass wall that stretches 200 feet wide and 60 feet tall, the plane looks like it's about to take flight through the window and over the rolling hills below.

Standing in the pavilion, I marveled at the exhilarating scene before me, nearly overwhelmed by the magnitude of emotions the sight elicited. I have visited countless airports and air force museums, yet nothing quite prepared me for the special experience of seeing and walking through the "White House on Wings" where so many powerful leaders have flown, worked, ate and slept. I spent about an hour in the pavilion, taking in the prominent aircraft along with a Marine One helicopter, an exhibit of Reagan's presidential motor-cade, and displays detailing the history of presidential aircraft over the years. I stepped out onto the pavilion's balcony for a few minutes to again admire the view of southern California, and then went back inside to check out the Ronald Reagan Pub. The pub, which was imported from Ireland in 2004, is where Ronald and Nancy Reagan enjoyed a toast and some hearty Irish hospitality on their visit to

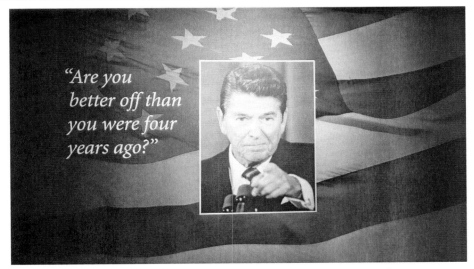

**Exhibit featuring Reagan's famous question posed
during his 1980 presidential campaign**

Ireland in 1984.

As I finished my tour and walked back to the parking lot, I reflected on all I had seen and experienced. There was no question that I had a far better understanding of and appreciation for the strong leadership and enduring legacy of Ronald Reagan—not only in the United States, but also around the world. He took office at a time when America desperately needed a strong and confident leader, and the world-changing impact he had can still be felt today. The Ronald Reagan Presidential Library and Museum is one historic place that I know I will visit again and again.

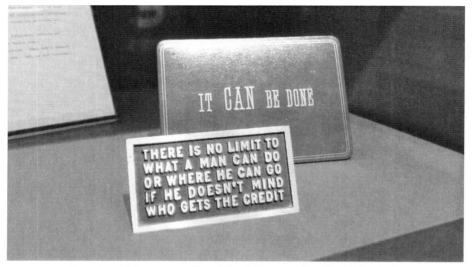

Two inspiring signs President Reagan kept on his desk

Exhibits depicting "The Reagan Strategy"—Peace Through Strength

Did You Know?

In the seven summers he spent as a lifeguard, young Ronald Reagan saved seventy-seven people from drowning. He also saved a swimmer's set of false teeth, for which he received a $10 tip!

Display showing President Reagan and Soviet leader Mikhail Gorbachev

Marine One helicopter used by Presidents Eisenhower through Ford

Did You Know?

After college graduation, one of Reagan's first jobs was as a radio sports announcer. His job included calling games for the Chicago Cubs—without actually attending the games. He would receive brief descriptions of plays over the wire and add colorful commentary, bringing the games to life for eager listeners.

Breathtaking view out the windows of the Air Force One Pavilion

Saddles and belt buckles from Reagan's collection

Did You Know?

Ronald Reagan loved jellybeans. For his first presidential inauguration Jelly Belly created a new flavor—blueberry. Over three tons of Jelly Belly beans were consumed during the inaugural festivities.

A portion of the Berlin Wall, just outside the museum

A bronze bust of the smiling Ronald Reagan

Did You Know?

At the time of his inauguration in 1981, Ronald Reagan was the oldest person to assume the presidency (he was sixty-nine).

The gravesite of Ronald Reagan

WHEN YOU VISIT...
DON'T MISS THESE:

- Flags of U.S. Presidents along the drive up the hill
- Spectacular panoramic views surrounding the library and museum
- Replicas of the White House South Lawn and Rose Garden
- Black Ace Squadron F-14A Fighter Jet
- Air Force One and presidential motorcade
- Gravesite of Ronald Reagan
- Replica of Reagan's Oval Office
- Great quotations throughout museum depicting Reagan's personal philosophies
- Gallery featuring Reagan's early life and career as a radio sports announcer and Hollywood actor
- Exhibits depicting Reagan's pivotal experience as a GE spokesman and the host of GE theater
- Exhibit featuring President Reagan's daily journal entries
- Display of Reagan's extensive personal collection of quotes

To see many more photos—in full color—please visit
www.presidentialleadershipbook.com/ronald-reagan/photos

"Freedom is never more than one generation away from extinction. We didn't pass it to our children in the bloodstream. It must be fought for, protected, and handed on for them to do the same."

"We can't help everyone, but everyone can help someone."

"There are no constraints on the human mind, no walls around the human spirit, no barriers to our progress except those we ourselves erect."

RONALD REAGAN
Affable, a Great Communicator, Poised, and *Pragmatic*

FULL NAME: Ronald Wilson Reagan
LIFESPAN: 93 years (1911 – 2004)
TERM: 40th President (R) 1981 – 1989

When Ronald Reagan left the White House in 1989, he left with one of the highest public approval ratings of an outgoing president in American history.[3] This remarkable leader was once described as "Optimistic but not naive. Articulate but not glib. Intelligent yet guided by common sense. Well mannered but never pretentious. Friendly but not a pushover. Charismatic but real. Principled but not intransigent. He was all of that and so much more."[4]

AFFABLE - showing warmth and friendliness; easy to approach and talk to; friendly, sociable, gregarious, likeable; cordial, gracious, pleasant.

Affable leaders put people at ease with their warmth and friendliness. Approachable and easy to talk to, they inspire trust and camaraderie among those they lead. Affable leaders have a knack for building relationships, garnering support, and earning the respect of others.

Always an entertainer, Reagan easily put people at ease and brought out a smile and a laugh. He learned from his mother, Nelle, to always look for the best in people, and as a persistent optimist, he looked for the silver lining in every situation. Even when he suffered a gunshot wound from a would-be assassin, he was still cracking jokes in the hospital and attempting to put everyone at ease, including his anxious wife, to whom he quipped, "Honey, I forgot to duck!"[5]

Born and raised in Illinois during the Great Depression, Ronald "Dutch" Reagan learned early the hardships of poverty and the value of hard work. His parents instilled in him strong principles and ideals; he learned from his mother the value of faith and prayer, and his father taught him the importance of tolerance and fair-treatment. Throughout his life Reagan exhibited idealism, strength, and goodness. One morning in May 1982, President Reagan read about a young family who had suffered racial prejudice in their predominately white neighborhood, including a cross burning in their yard by the Ku Klux Klan. Angered by the news story, Reagan resolved to pay the family a visit to show his concern for them and to make a statement about the reprehensible nature of such harassment. His surprise visit to the Maryland suburb made a lasting impression on the victimized family and the entire community.

President Reagan sincerely enjoyed the company of others and possessed an innate ability to connect with people. He was naturally sociable and outgoing, but after the failed attempt on his life just two months into his presidency, he experienced a sudden shift in his way of life. Protective measures no longer allowed him to engage crowds and "meet and greet" as he was so fond of. The president became all but walled-off by his protective detail, which sapped much of his previously gregarious spirit. Reflecting on his presidency, Reagan said wistfully, "You spend a lot of time going by too fast in a car someone else is driving and seeing the people through tinted glass— the parents holding up a child and the wave you saw too late and couldn't return. And so many times I wanted to stop and reach out from behind the glass and connect."[6]

GREAT COMMUNICATOR – able to effectively communicate meaning, intention and passion both verbally and nonverbally; eloquent, articulate, expressive; compelling, influential, inspiring.

Great communicators are able to effectively communicate not only through their words, gestures, facial expressions and careful timing, but also through their decisions and actions. They realize that everything they say and do communicates a message, and they leverage that knowledge to their advantage. Leaders who are great communicators carefully weigh every word and measure each decision to ensure they are conveying their true intended meaning and purpose.

Often referred to as "The Great Communicator," Ronald Reagan was a talented orator with experience dating back to his schooldays. His communication and leadership skills steadily improved in high school as he participated in sports and school plays and served as the student body president. While at Eureka College as a young man, Reagan continued to participate extensively in athletics as well as in the drama and debate clubs. He was also a reporter for the college newspaper, helped edit the yearbook, and served as president of the student council. During his freshman year he represented his peers in a rousing speech as part of a student strike in protest of faculty layoffs and budget cuts. His ability to connect with and inspire people and to convey his vision quickly became evident as he became more and more experienced with public address.

After college Reagan became a radio sports announcer with a flair for entertainment, and a few years later he debuted as a Hollywood actor. He enjoyed a successful acting career in Hollywood over the next two decades, appearing in fifty-two films including *Knute Rockne* and *The King's Row*, which featured some of his best performances. As his acting career wound down, he signed a contract with General Electric to be a host for the TV show, *General Electric Theater*, and more significantly, serve as a GE spokesman who visited and spoke with employees at factories across the country.

His eight years with GE provided Reagan with a unique opportunity to meet with and speak to large crowds of working-class Americans; by the time he left GE he had visited each of its 139 plants at least once, and had spoken to over 250,000 GE employees. This proved to be a transformational period of Reagan's life, during which time he began to be more politically minded. He gradually moved away from entertainment and toward a future of political activism, speaking to small groups or crowds of hundreds, always in his eloquent, dramatic style delicately weighted with both fervency and wit. It became clear to everyone who listened to his inspiring and persuasive speeches that Ronald Reagan was a power to be reckoned with. Here was a man who not only spoke well, but also spoke with substance; in the words of the Great Communicator himself, "Most often it's not how handsomely or eloquently you say something, but the fact that your words mean something."[7]

POISED – possessing self-confidence, control, and steady composure; dignified, confident, self-assured, graceful.

Leaders with poise are not often hindered by self-doubt or insecurity. Self-assured and composed, they demonstrate steady self-control and cool-headed decision making. Dignified and gracious, poised leaders often have a calming presence that sets people at ease and inspires confidence.

Ronald Reagan possessed great self-assurance and poise. Comfortable with who he was without being arrogant or self-centered, he was an easygoing man who exuded confidence in both speech and composure. Even in the "party-world" of Hollywood, Reagan remained true to himself, standing out from many of his colleagues as being uncommonly moral, refraining from the self-indulgence and debauchery typical of his peers.

A natural leader, Reagan possessed the ability to remain cool and calm in the face of opposition. During the presidential campaign of 1980, his calm temperament gave Reagan a clear advantage over his opponent, Jimmy Carter, who tended to be easily provoked and would become defensive. During a televised debate shortly before Election Day, Reagan famously chuckled in response to some of Carter's criticisms, remarking, "There you go again"[8]—a line that went down in history books and further endeared Reagan to the American public.

As governor of California and later as the president, Reagan demonstrated steady resolve, willing to make tough decisions and stand behind them. During his first year as president, Reagan was challenged by an illegal strike of nearly twelve thousand air traffic controllers that severely hampered air traffic across the nation. In describing his response to that challenge, Reagan explained,

> *This episode was an early test of my administration's resolve. We had the choice of caving in to unreasonable demands while keeping our air traffic system operating without incident, or taking a stand for what we thought was right with the risk of throwing the system into possible chaos. I felt we had to do what was right... I think the principle was worth the price.[9]*

President Reagan later showed that same resolve during his famous speech in front of the Berlin Wall in June of 1987. Overriding the advice of his foreign policy advisors, who strongly urged him to reconsider the words of his speech, Reagan uttered a momentous challenge to the General Secretary of the Soviet Union, Mikhail Gorbachev. The president's advisors feared he would jeopardize the pivotal but delicate diplomatic relationship he had forged with Gorbachev. Nonetheless, Reagan was resolved, and with characteristic confidence, he delivered each word with force: "Mr. Gorbachev, tear down this wall!"[10] Remarkably, Gorbachev accepted the challenge from this bold American president, and twenty-nine months later, the wall came down.

—◦✦◦—

PRAGMATIC - approaching situations with a practical mindset and utilizing common sense; adopting practical measures to solve problems; sensible, judicious, thoughtful.

Leaders with a pragmatic outlook tend to be straightforward and practical. Decisive and realistic, they base their decisions on facts and simple logic, weighing the pros and cons and then choosing the path that makes the most sense to them. Pragmatic leaders desire practical solutions, and they tend to understand the value and importance of working together to reach the most desirable outcome.

Throughout his life, Reagan practiced an optimistic but pragmatic approach to leadership. He was practical minded, guided by common sense and making choices that he felt were logical and the outcomes of which would be most beneficial long-term.

Reagan was a Democrat for the first half of his life, but his political ideology shifted over time. As his life circumstances changed, he came to identify more and more with the Republican Party, and in 1962 he officially switched his party registration. As a Republican governor and president, Reagan was not afraid to make bipartisan compromises in order to accomplish key goals. Though his fellow Republicans didn't always appreciate his blurring of political lines, Reagan understood the importance of working together to come to reasonable resolutions. Even with this practical outlook, he still fought with Congress on much of his proposed legislation, once joking, "I have wondered at times what the Ten Commandments would have looked like if Moses had run them through the U.S. Congress."

Ronald Reagan was a dedicated leader, but he also understood the importance of balancing his workload with rest and family time. The president knew, as did his family and his White House aides, that he worked best when he was well rested and had time to relax. He enjoyed regular visits to his ranch in California, known as Rancho del Cielo, with First Lady Nancy Reagan. The president joked, "It's true hard work never killed anybody, but I figure, why take the chance?"[11] Though he poked fun at himself and his frequent working vacations, Reagan shouldered the responsibilities of his office with determination and perseverance; he worked hard, but he also wisely allowed himself leisure time. Reagan's practical outlook on work, life, and leadership enabled him to lead the nation with steadiness and understanding.

11

GEORGE BUSH
PRESIDENTIAL LIBRARY & MUSEUM
College Station, Texas

The George Bush Presidential Library and Museum is located on a beautiful ninety-acre piece of land on the campus of Texas A&M University in College Station, Texas. When I arrived on campus I turned onto Barbara Bush Drive, wound through the spacious grounds, and soon pulled into the parking lot. As I walked toward the buildings, my eyes were immediately drawn to the front of the museum, where a brightly painted bench featuring Old Glory sits front and center. Just behind the bench, surrounding a bubbling fountain, are eight American flags, offering a proud and inspiring red, white, and blue welcome. The stately elegance and symmetry catches the eye and gives the place a very 'presidential' feel.

To the left of the entrance, I could not help but notice a unique sculpture that momentarily distracted me from the museum. I got closer for a better look, and was awed by the sight of five magnificent bronze horses glinting in the bright sunlight as they leap over a

"The Day the Wall Came Down"—a symbol of freedom

replica of the fallen Berlin Wall. By reading the inscription at its base, I learned that the captivating sculpture is called "The Day the Wall Came Down," a monument to freedom by artist Veryl Goodnight.

After admiring and photographing the sculpture for several minutes, I made my way inside, where I spent the next five hours exploring the wonders of America as it was from the 1920s through Bush's presidency and years as an elder statesman. The museum beautifully features the life and times of my fellow American, George Herbert Walker Bush, who grew up to be president. Through stunning displays and interactive exhibits, the story and legacy of President Bush are artfully preserved. From Bush family photos to personal letters to an actual torpedo bomber hanging from the ceiling, the museum is chalk-full of treasures you won't find anywhere else. I truly experienced the story of the forty-first U.S. President like never before, learning about his strong faith, family values, and commitment to lifelong service.

After completing my tour, I headed outside to explore the rest of the grounds. Hidden behind the museum I found a quiet pond, about two acres in size, reflecting the fading sunlight. I walked around the pond and strolled through the Barbara Bush Rose Garden, enjoying the beautiful, peaceful setting. Crossing a small footbridge on

Exhibits depicting the Bush family values and traditions

the far side of the pond, I walked down a winding path through the trees to a small clearing. Here I found the gravesite of Robin, the Bushes' precious little girl who died of leukemia shortly before what would have been her fourth birthday. Not yet needed, her parents' final resting places are reserved by Robin's side. I was moved by the tragic loss of such a little girl to the terrible monster of cancer, and reminded of the Bushes' enduring commitment to the work being done to conquer the disease.

As the shadows grew longer and the sunshine turned golden, I retraced my steps back to the front of the museum. I paused for a few minutes to again reflect in front of the sculpture that had drawn my attention when I first arrived. I had learned and experienced so much in the seven hours I'd spent at the museum and grounds. I was intrigued and impressed by the life and times of President Bush, and inspired by the legacy that he has created and that this fascinating museum preserves. What a treasure of American history!

Exhibit depicting young George Bush's service in the naval air force during World War II

The baseball mitt used by Bush at Yale and later kept in his Oval Office

Did You Know?

George Bush enlisted in the navy on his eighteenth birthday, just six months after the attack on Pearl Harbor. At the time of his commission, he was the youngest naval aviator in navy history.

1947 Studebaker identical to the one Bush drove to Texas in 1948

Sculpture and exhibits representing Bush's time as Ambassador to the U.N.

Did You Know?

George Bush celebrated his seventy-fifth, eightieth, and eighty-fifth birthdays by skydiving. His very first parachute jump was when he was a twenty-year-old navy pilot and his plane was shot down during a World War II bombing mission.

Gallery featuring the Bushes' experience living in China

A portion of an exhibit depicting the Persian Gulf War

Did You Know?

George and Barbara Bush lived in China for two years while he was serving as the chief of the U.S. liaison office in China. Though they were provided a Chrysler sedan for transportation, the Bushes chose to break the traditional mold of American envoys and instead "travel as the Chinese do"—on bicycles.

Barbara Bush Rose Garden overlooking a large pond behind the museum

Bridge and pathway leading to the Bush family gravesite

Did You Know?

George and Barbara Bush are the longest married presidential couple. Wed on January 6, 1945, they have enjoyed more than sixty-eight years of marriage. A few years after their wedding, George Bush wrote to a friend, "I haven't had the chance to make many shrewd moves in my young life, but when I married Bar, I hit the proverbial jackpot."[1]

Eventual gravesite of the Bushes, alongside their daughter Robin

WHEN YOU VISIT...
DON'T MISS THESE:

- The spacious and peaceful grounds surrounding the library and museum, including the pond, rose garden, and gravesite
- Sculpture of horses leaping over the fallen Berlin Wall
- Gallery featuring Bush's service as a navy pilot
- Photographs and quotes portraying Bush's faith, family and friends
- Exhibits detailing the years Bush spent at Yale after the war
- Restored 1947 Studebaker
- Exhibits depicting Bush's successful and varied political career, from congressman to president
- Collection of presidential gifts of state
- Replica of Bush's Camp David office
- Replica of the White House Situation Room
- Extensive Gulf War exhibits
- Exhibits featuring the service and many accomplishments of First Lady Barbara Bush

To see many more photos—in full color—please visit
www.presidentialleadershipbook.com/george-h-w-bush/photos

"I have tried to keep my mind open to what other people think, even if I disagree... that's an element of leadership—not just talking, but listening."

"I see history as a book with many pages, and each day we fill a page with acts of hopefulness and meaning."

"Use power to help people. For we are given power not to advance our own purposes, nor to make a great show in the world, nor a name. There is but one just use of power and it is to serve people."

GEORGE H. W. BUSH
Team Player, Steadfast, Committed to Service,
and *Compassionate*

FULL NAME: George Herbert Walker Bush
LIFESPAN: 89+ years (1924 –)
TERM: 41st President (R) 1989 – 1993

George H. W. Bush is a leader with a wide range of experience. At various times in his life Bush served as a World War II combat pilot, captain of the Yale baseball team, independent Texas oilman, U.S. congressman, ambassador to the U.N., chairman of the Republican National Committee, chief of the U.S. liaison office in China, director of the CIA, vice president, and ultimately, the forty-first President of the United States. Bush's diverse background shaped him into a president with a truly unique view of the world.

TEAM PLAYER – gladly working in cooperation with others; eagerly joining with others to work for a common purpose or goal; modest; not egocentric or overly concerned with self-promotion; dealing civilly with others, including opponents; diplomatic, respectful, considerate, fair.

Leaders who are team players realize they can only accomplish so much on their own, and they recognize the immense value and importance of working together. With little concern for who gets the credit for success, team players focus on contributing their best for the benefit of all.

George Bush was blessed with parents who embodied a spirit of public service and a commitment to traditional values. Like his parents, young Bush enjoyed and excelled at sports, and he learned from their example to put the best interests of the team above his own. If he told his mother about the goals he scored in soccer, she would always ask him how the team as a whole did; "My mother loved games and thought competition taught courage, fair play, and—I think most importantly—teamwork."[2] Bush was well liked and quickly became popular among his classmates at Phillips Academy in Andover, Massachusetts. A diligent student and talented athlete, Bush served as chairman of student deacons, president of his senior class, and captain of the soccer and baseball teams. Friends at school quipped that Bush was good at anything that had a ball attached to it, and a classmate at Yale later said of Bush, "Everything he did he did well."[3]

As he grew up, Bush continued to value teamwork, cooperation, and personal modesty. He took these values with him when he joined the navy on his eighteenth birthday, and he demonstrated them after the war as a student at Yale. He continued to excel in sports while in college, serving as captain of Yale's varsity baseball team. He had the privilege of meeting Babe Ruth while at Yale, though his baseball idol was actually Lou Gehrig, who Bush admired for his "standard of excellence on and off the field. Nothing flashy, no hotdogging, the ideal sportsman."[4] Bush made it his goal to model that standard of excellence and sportsmanship throughout his life.

George Bush's reluctance to "toot his own horn" or denigrate his opponents sometimes proved to be a handicap in his political career. At the urging of campaign aides and consultants, Bush reluctantly went against his nature and upbringing in order to bolster his campaign efforts, but he was never comfortable with self-promoting tactics. He has never been a performer—often awkward in front of crowds and when interacting with the press—but he has always been a people person. As president, behind closed doors George Bush was a warm and generous man who nurtured deep friendships and made strong personal connections with political leaders and heads of state across the world. He was known to pick up the phone and call foreign leaders without any political agenda in mind, but just to say, "Hello," and, "How are you?" Bush is a man with innate diplomacy. For him, building and maintaining relationships as president wasn't merely about political networking, but was something he genuinely enjoyed and cared about.

It was this diplomacy and ability to connect with others that helped President Bush pave the way to America's success in the Persian Gulf War. Upon word of Iraq's invasion of Kuwait, sanctioned by Iraqi president, Saddam Hussein, President Bush leapt into action. He worked tirelessly to build a coalition of world leaders who would unite and stand opposed to Iraq's military aggression and subsequent atrocities it committed against the people of Kuwait. Bush and the leaders of the United Nations earnestly sought a peaceful resolution to the conflict, but the situation came to a head when Iraq refused to withdraw from Kuwait despite an ultimatum from the UN. With the support of the United Nations and the U.S. Congress, President Bush authorized use of military force against Iraq. In the ensuing war, known as the Gulf War or Operation Desert Storm, coalition forces drove out Iraqi invaders in less than two months. In wake of this decisive victory, President Bush's approval rating topped out at eighty-nine percent—a record high that wasn't beat until ten years later by the forty-third U.S. President, his son George W. Bush.[5]

STEADFAST - firm in purpose or direction; resolved, unwavering, resolute; holding fast to principles or convictions; faithful, loyal, committed.

Steadfast leaders are dependable and trustworthy. Firm in their decisions and set in purpose, they faithfully fulfill their responsibilities and hold fast to their convictions. Steadfast leaders are neither hesitant to try new things nor eager to enact radical change, instead they pursue a balance of continuity and progress.

George Bush was raised in a cultured and affluent family in Greenwich, Connecticut. His father, Prescott Bush, was an investment banker who was involved in local politics and later became a Republican senator. Though his family was wealthy, young George Bush and his siblings were raised to be modest, appreciate their blessings, and to give back to society. Like his father, George Bush grew up to be a conservative man who approached life's pursuits with caution but steady commitment. When he started to feel the political itch in the early 1960s, Bush was an oilman in Texas. His first major step into politics was as the chairman of the Harris County Republican Committee in Houston, Texas. As a politician, Bush certainly wasn't afraid of change and adventure, but he also saw the value of slow and steady progress, often choosing a path of continuity rather than radical change.

George Bush approached big decisions with caution and much forethought, but when he did determine to do something, he was steadfast. Whether it was joining the navy as a youth, moving his new family across the country, quitting his job to start his own oil business, running for Congress, moving to China, or any other decision, when George Bush made up his mind to do something, he pursued it wholeheartedly no matter the challenges.

One of the first major political decisions George Bush had to make was regarding civil rights. One element of the Civil Rights Act of 1968 was a fair housing bill that would ban racial discrimination in housing. The bill came to the floor for a vote in April of 1968. At the time, Bush was a Republican representative from Texas, and many of his constituents were vehemently opposed to the bill that the

Democratic president, Lyndon B. Johnson, had put before Congress. Bush was put in a difficult position with a big decision to make. He had previously campaigned in opposition to certain civil rights legislation and knew it was what his constituents expected, but at his core George Bush believed in equality. As was his nature, Bush did not take this decision lightly; "You've got to wrestle with your conscience. You've got to listen to people. It doesn't come so easy to me that this is right and that's wrong. It's never that simple. The tough votes are the ones you agonize over and then you do what you think is right."[6] Ultimately, after weighing the pros and cons against his own personal convictions, Bush made the decision that he felt was right and voted in favor of the controversial bill.

The outrage and feeling of betrayal within his district was significant, but Bush stood behind his decision with firm conviction, appearing before a hostile crowd of booing and hissing constituents to explain his vote. Bush stood tall before the angry audience, and borrowing from philosopher Edmund Burke, said, "Your representative owes you not only his industry, but his judgment; and he betrays, instead of serving you, if he sacrifices his judgment to your opinion." He went on to say, "I voted from conviction, not out of intimidation or fear… but because of a feeling deep down in my heart that this was the right thing for me to do."[7] George Bush's speech that night was one of the most dramatic events of his political career. By calmly explaining his decision and the personal conviction behind it, Congressman Bush worked his way out of a precarious situation and left the stage that night not to the boos of the crowd, but to resounding applause.

⸜⌒ᦁ⌒⸝

COMMITTED TO SERVICE - personally compelled to serve others; possessing a motivating awareness of ethical and civic responsibility; dutiful, patriotic, servant-hearted.

Leaders who are committed to service feel a sense of responsibility for the state of the world and the welfare of others. They desire to use their unique skills, background, and experience to help improve the world around them and to further worthy causes.

Thanks to his parents' social status and wealth, Bush enjoyed a comfortable upbringing, shielded from many of the hardships of the Great Depression that so many Americans endured. However, the Bush children were not spoiled, and as a child little George Bush earned the nickname "Have Half" because of his tendency to offer half of whatever he had to his siblings and friends.

George Bush was raised to possess a sense of duty to society and to his country, and from the time he was a young man he has demonstrated a commitment to service. Presidential historian John Robert Greene explains that Bush's father "wanted his children to understand that there was a world beyond the boundaries of Greenwich, and that they were expected to give something back to that world, whether it be through business, whether it be through public service, or whether it be through military service."[8] As a teenager with a strong sense of patriotism, and spurred on by the Japanese attack on Pearl Harbor in December 1941, George Bush chose military service as one way to give back to the world.

He enlisted in the navy the day he graduated from high school, which happened to be his eighteenth birthday. One year later he was commissioned as the youngest pilot in the naval air service, and in December 1943 he was assigned to the USS *San Jacinto* in the Pacific Ocean. The young pilot spent the next year flying an Avenger bomber he named *Barbara* after his girl back home. In September 1944, Bush's plane was shot down during a bombing raid over a small Japanese island. The twenty-year-old pilot was the only survivor of his three-man crew—a heavy burden that still weighs on his mind more than sixty years later.

After the end of the war and his discharge from the navy, Bush got a college degree from Yale University, and then entered the Texas oil business. In the early 1960s he first began actively pursuing public office, following in his father's footsteps and renewing his commitment to serve his community and his country. Over the course of the next three and a half decades Bush did just that, gladly serving his nation and fellow Americans in a wide array of positions. His political career began in Texas with his role as the chairman of the Harris County Republican Committee, and it culminated in his service as the forty-first President of the United States. Bush believes that, "There is but one just use of power, and it is to serve people."[9] It is this conviction that led him to advocate voluntarism, vote in favor of the civil rights fair housing bill, and use his power as the President of the United States to offer aid to the people of Kuwait in the face of Iraqi aggression.

As an elder statesman, Bush continues to use his influence and follow in his parents' footsteps serving others, believing that, "To serve and to serve well is the highest fulfillment we can know."[10] President Barack Obama once gave this description of the forty-first U.S. President:

> George Bush isn't just a president who promoted the ethic of service long before it was fashionable; he's a citizen whose life has embodied that ethic. From his daring service as a navy pilot during World War II, enlisting the day he turned eighteen, to his time in Congress, at the CIA, as UN Ambassador, Vice President and President. He easily could have chosen a life of comfort and privilege, but instead, time and again, when offered a chance to serve, he seized it. It was second nature to him—the continuation of a proud family tradition that he and Mrs. Bush clearly passed on to their children and grandchildren, and one that he has carried on throughout his "retirement"... working tirelessly to help others, without fanfare or any expectation or desire for recognition.[11]

⟨⟩∘⟨⟩

COMPASSIONATE - possessing and demonstrating a feeling of deep empathy, understanding, or sorrow for those who are stricken by misfortune; sympathetic, kindhearted, tender.

Compassionate leaders possess a clear understanding of the depths and impact of human emotion. They realize that at the end of the day, everyone is human, and everyone has sorrows and joys, setbacks and triumphs. Compassionate leaders are perceptive and empathetic to the needs and concerns of others, and deal with people with kindness and understanding.

George Bush married his high school sweetheart, Barbara Pierce, while on leave from the navy in January 1945. Following Japanese surrender and the end of the war, he was honorably discharged, and soon afterwards the young couple started a family. By the spring of 1953 the Bush family had grown by three— George Walker, Pauline Robinson "Robin," and John Ellis "Jeb." Just a few weeks after baby Jeb arrived, the Bushes received terrible news—three-year-old Robin was diagnosed with Leukemia. The Bushes did all they could to fight for the life of their little girl, but just two months before what would have been her fourth birthday, the cancer claimed Robin's life. Her parents' grief was raw and palpable. Bush said of that time, "Barbara and I sustained each other; but in the end, it was our faith that truly sustained us."[12]

Over the next several years the family grew by two more boys, but there remained a void that couldn't be filled. In the late 1950s, Bush wrote a poignant letter to his mother,

> *There is about our house a need... We need some starched crisp frocks to go with all our torn-kneed blue jeans and helmets. We need some soft blond hair to offset those crew cuts. We need a doll house to stand firm against our forts and rackets and thousand baseball cards... We need a legitimate Christmas angel—one who doesn't have cuffs beneath the dress. We need someone who's afraid of frogs. We need someone to cry when I get mad—not argue. We need a little one who can kiss without leaving egg or jam or gum. We need a girl.[13]*

On August 18, 1959, the Bushes' second daughter and youngest child, Dorothy "Doro" Bush, was born. At the hospital after her birth, George Bush leaned his head against the nursery glass and wept.

This tender, emotional, and compassionate side of George Bush has not often been seen by the American public. Biographer

Timothy Naftali explains that Bush is reluctant to publicly show his emotions, believing that, "That's not what a man did—a man of his generation and of his upbringing."[14] Though he often appeared stoic and restrained in the public eye, President Bush possessed great compassion. The suffering he observed during the Great Depression and World War II and the grief he experienced after the loss of his crewmen and the loss of his daughter shaped George Bush into an empathetic and understanding man who possesses sure convictions about helping others. This compassion, along with his commitment to service, steadfast resolve, and ability to work well with others, has equipped George Bush as an effective and admirable leader who has built an enduring legacy of servant leadership.

12

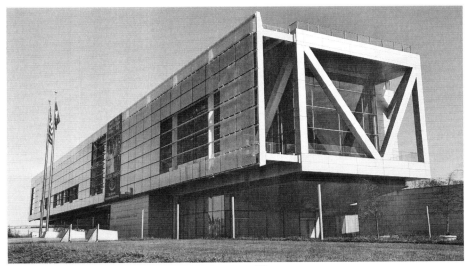

WILLIAM J. CLINTON
PRESIDENTIAL LIBRARY & MUSEUM
Little Rock, Arkansas

I always enjoy my trips to Little Rock, Arkansas, a city brimming with rich and colorful American history. Nestled on the banks of the Arkansas River, old mixes with new in this diverse state capital, with ornate Victorian buildings neighboring shiny skyscrapers made of glass and steel. The Clinton Presidential Center and Park, located right next to Little Rock's popular river market district, fits well in the city's culture that mixes the legacy of history with the promise of tomorrow.

The riverfront park includes a restored historic train station that now houses the University of Arkansas Clinton School of Public Service and the Little Rock offices of the Clinton Foundation. A stone's throw from the historic redbrick building is the presidential library and museum, built over one hundred years later. The large modern-looking glass and steel structure is very much a building of the future. Reflecting Clinton's 1996 campaign slogan, "Building a

Converted railroad bridge now used as a footbridge across the river

bridge to the twenty-first century," the building's design is bridge-like, reaching toward the far shore of the Arkansas river, and symbolically bridging the gap between yesterday and tomorrow.

On one trip to Little Rock, I stayed a couple days in my motorhome just across the river from the presidential center and park. A renovated railroad bridge, now serving as a popular footbridge, allowed me easy access to the park across the river. As I approached the library and museum, I was intrigued by the contrast between the historic architecture of the old railroad bridge under my feet and the modern design of the building in front of me, perched on the bank of the river. In contrast to some of the other presidential libraries and museums—such as the fortress-like and nearly windowless LBJ Library—from the outside, the Clinton Library and Museum appears to be made up almost entirely of windows. As soon as I walked inside, I noticed with appreciation the open feeling of the large sunlit building. I later learned that the Clinton Library and Museum is the first federal building—and one of only a few dozens buildings in the world—to receive the highest rating available from the Leadership in Energy and Environmental Design (LEED) green building certification program.[1]

The layout of the museum is very simple and efficient; the tour

View out the museum windows toward downtown Little Rock

starts on the second floor with a replica Oval Office and an inter-active Cabinet Room. Then, instead of winding through a maze of exhibits, I found myself in a large, open gallery that encompasses both the second and third floors of the museum. The lower level of the gallery features a comprehensive timeline of Clinton's years in office. I slowly made my way down the timeline, intrigued by the details of Clinton's administration, as depicted through text and interactive audio-visual displays on each of the eight large panels that line the center of the room. Along each side of the timeline are alcoves with more information about significant events, complete with intriguing inside stories and hundreds of exclusive photos.

After perusing the lower half of the gallery, I proceeded upstairs to the third floor, where I explored additional exhibits and admired a collection of gifts that President Clinton received on behalf of America. The diverse gifts on exhibit range from unique items given by admiring American citizens—such as a restored 1946 Schwinn bicycle with the name "Mr. President" emblazoned on the side—to elaborate gifts from foreign heads of state, like ornately decorated swords and figures made from precious stones. I slowly made my way through each exhibit, enjoying seeing the unique items bestowed upon the forty-second president in this long-standing tradition of

Main exhibit gallery

diplomacy and goodwill.

When I finally emerged from the museum late that afternoon, the shadows were already getting long and the setting sun bathed the grounds in golden light. As I walked away from the presidential center and back across the footbridge, I felt inspired by the presidential legacy preserved there, and by the center's mission to make an enduring global impact by equipping a new generation of leaders. President Clinton's commitment to public service is truly embodied by this fascinating presidential center that bears his name.

President Clinton's desk within Oval Office replica

Replica of White House Cabinet Room

Did You Know?
Bill Clinton's biological father was killed in an auto accident three months before Bill was born.

Timeline featuring each year of Clinton's presidency

Example table setting for official State Dinners

Did You Know?

In high school Bill Clinton played saxophone in a jazz trio, which was known as the "Three Blind Mice" due to the dark glasses the boys wore. He still plays the saxophone to this day.

One of many gifts of state accepted by President Clinton

Specially restored 1946 Schwinn bicycle given to President Clinton

Did You Know?

In the 1970s Bill Clinton met Steven Spielberg, who at that time was an unknown television director. They have remained friends ever since, and Clinton even made a surprise appearance at the 2013 Golden Globes to introduce the film "Lincoln," which was directed by the now world-famous Spielberg.

Clinton's presidential limousine

View of the library and museum from across the Arkansas River

Did You Know?

Bill Clinton was the first president to win a Grammy—for best spoken word album in 2004 (Wolf Tracks) and again in 2005 (My Life).

Clinton School of Public Affairs housed inside historic railroad station

Pathway through restored wetlands adjacent to Clinton Presidential Park

Did You Know?
Bill Clinton was the first Democratic president since Franklin Roosevelt to win a second term in office.

Clinton's first home, located in Hope, Arkansas

WHEN YOU VISIT...
DON'T MISS THESE:

- Clinton Presidential Park and the converted railroad footbridge spanning the Arkansas River
- Clinton School of Public Affairs housed inside historic Choctaw Route railroad station
- William E. "Bill" Clark Presidential Park Wetlands
- Replica of Clinton's Oval Office
- Replica of the White House Cabinet Room
- Clinton's presidential limousine
- Collection of gifts of state
- Each of the alcoves depicting the eight years of Clinton's administration
- "Forty-Two" Restaurant overlooking Arkansas River
- Nearby museum store
- Clinton home in Hope, Arkansas

To see many more photos—in full color—please visit
www.presidentialleadershipbook.com/bill-clinton/photos

"If you live long enough, you'll make mistakes. But if you learn from them, you'll be a better person. It's how you handle adversity, not how it affects you. The main thing is never quit, never quit, never quit."

"Promising too much can be as cruel as caring too little."

"When we give what we can and give it with joy, we don't just renew the American tradition of giving, we also renew ourselves."

BILL CLINTON
Focused, Engaging, and *Resilient*

FULL NAME: William Jefferson Clinton
LIFESPAN: 67+ years (1946 –)
TERM: 42nd President (D) 1993 – 2001

Probably no other president in history has weathered the kind of storms and public scandal that President William Jefferson Clinton did during his time in office. A man of great ambition and irresistible charisma, arguably his most significant leadership quality was his steadfast perseverance and ability to rebound from setbacks.

FOCUSED – intent on a particular direction or goal; not easily distracted or deterred; determined, resolved, ambitious.

Leaders with great focus know exactly where they want to go and are determined to get there. Intent on their goal, they celebrate small successes but always keep the end in mind, quickly returning their attention to their priority objective. Focused leaders are not easily distracted or deterred, and they usually excel at keeping those whom they lead on track to success.

William Jefferson Blythe was born to be a politician. It wasn't until he was a teenager that young Bill took his stepfather's last name, but he was already shaping the future that would put the name Bill Clinton in the history books. As a boy, Clinton's mother told him he would one day be president, and as he grew up, the dream of a doting parent began to take shape into a personal vision. Years later, political advisor Carol Willis said of Clinton, "I think he was born with political ambition. And I think that he was using every step of his life as a classroom to build the foundation to where he ultimately wanted to go."[2]

Clinton excelled in school and fostered a growing passion for politics. In 1963, seventeen-year-old Clinton had the opportunity to travel to Washington, D.C. as an Arkansas delegate to Boys Nation—an elite nonpartisan program designed to introduce selected youth to the processes of the federal government. While there, Clinton shook hands with President John F. Kennedy in a moment famously preserved in history by the snap of a reporter's camera. Young Clinton returned home to Hot Springs, Arkansas determined more than ever to pursue that most coveted executive position.

The starry-eyed youth who shook hands with President Kennedy graduated from high school in 1964 and went on to Georgetown University, where he majored in international affairs and became very active in student government. While in college Clinton began working as a clerk for the Foreign Relations Committee of the U.S. Senate, which helped to further shape his political temperament. As a testament to Clinton's affinity for political and scholastic achievement, while finishing his senior year at Georgetown he was awarded the prestigious Rhodes Scholarship to attend Oxford University in England for two years. After Oxford, Clinton went on to earn a law degree from Yale, and then moved back to his home state where he started teaching law at the University of Arkansas and began planning his launch into politics.

In addition to earning his law degree while at Yale, Clinton had also secured the life-long political and personal partnership that would endure the unimaginable turbulence of his future career in public service. Hillary Rodham was an intellectual and driven young law student who attracted the attention of the ambitious Bill Clinton. Together, the couple became a political force to be reckoned with, sharing a passion for public service and each fostering a deep-seated desire to one day attain the presidency. Historian William Chafe described the couple as having "a common sense of commitment to social justice, of working on improving the lives of families, of being concerned about the disenfranchised. But ultimately all along, thinking about going to the top."[3] They were married in a private ceremony in 1975, and with the strong support and partnership of his wife behind him, Clinton began his political climb.

～◦ゞ◦～

ENGAGING - actively capturing the attention and involvement of others; dynamic, appealing, charming, charismatic, alluring, pleasing.

Engaging leaders are dynamic and energetic, actively connecting with people and building relationships. They are sociable and charming, eager to meet and get to know people. Far from remaining isolated or aloof, engaging leaders enjoy the company of others and seek involvement in whatever is going on.

Bill Clinton's first foray into politics was his 1974 campaign for a seat in the U.S. House of Representatives against incumbent John Paul Hammerschmidt. Though he lost the election, it was by a surprisingly small margin for a bid from a twenty-eight-year-old with no experience in public office. The measure of success that Clinton experienced during this first campaign undoubtedly correlated with his relentless energy and his ability to charm and connect with people. Clinton possessed natural political acumen and an innate charisma that wowed observers. Gubernatorial campaign aide Bobby Roberts described Clinton as having an "extra battery," explaining, "He would just keep going. We might stop at a service station or restaurant or whatever, and he would want to meet the cooks. He would go back in the kitchen and meet everybody back there. He would not leave a place, I think, where he had not met everyone."[4] Clinton's first congressional bid, though unsuccessful, established him as a rising star of the local Democratic Party.

Two years after losing the congressional race, Clinton was elected state attorney general, and in 1978 went on to become governor. At thirty-two he was one of the youngest governors in American history. As governor, Clinton pursued an ambitious agenda, desiring to solve his state's woes in one fell swoop. Unfortunately, his well-intentioned attempts to transform the state all at once proved to be overambitious and caused Clinton's constituents to doubt his ability to govern. After just one two-year term, he lost his bid for reelection. Clinton was devastated by the defeat and worried that it might signal the end of his political career. However, he learned from his mistakes, and with the help of his wife, launched a remarkable comeback campaign. The charming young politician readily admitted to the public that he had made some poor decisions as governor the first time, and promised that if they gave him a second chance, it would be different. Instead of trying to fix all of the state's problems, he narrowed his focus to one thing everyone supported: improving education. His campaign worked, and just two years after leaving the governorship in defeat, Clinton was back, this time for four consecutive terms.

Clinton loved his state, and thoroughly enjoyed being governor. The governorship reinforced his passion for serving in public office, and it helped to propel him toward the presidency. Clinton's charisma was a major advantage that helped position him for a very bright political future, but not only was he incredibly charming, he was also politically savvy. Political consultant Dick Morris described

Clinton's time as governor:

> *He would spend a huge amount of time meeting with, impressing,*
> *and charming his fellow governors and other elected officials, and after*
> *a day and a night with him talking about philosophy and politics,*
> *you came away with the impression that this was the smartest guy in*
> *the class, and that essentially if you were going to have a president, it*
> *probably should be this guy.*[5]

Clinton's charisma got him in the door, but it was his intelligence and political savvy that kept him there.

~◠◡◠~

RESILIENT - able to withstand or bounce back from adversity; quick to recover; buoyant, spirited, irrepressible, energetic, hardy, persevering.

Resilient leaders are hardy and tough-skinned, able to endure adversity, setbacks, criticism, opposition, or even disgrace. No matter what kind of hits they take or falls they experience, resilient leaders bounce back and keep going with renewed energy and determination.

By the end of the 1980s, some were already considering Clinton as a prospective presidential candidate, though he chose to hold off his bid for office until the 1992 election. During his last term as governor he continued to hone his national image, emerging as one of the leading reform Democrats. However, he made a political gaffe in 1988 during a televised speech in support of democratic presidential nominee Michael Dukakis. Though he would be later known for his powerful oratorical skills, that evening at the Democratic National Convention Clinton came across as long-winded and boring, famously getting the loudest round of applause when he said, "In closing..." However, once again Clinton's irrepressible charisma saved him when he compensated for his blunder by deftly poking fun at himself during a quickly arranged appearance on the *Tonight Show*. Producer and director Harry Thomason, a friend of Clinton's, marveled, "In an instant, he had turned it around, because the next day papers were full of good things, and had kind things to say about him, and so it erased almost all of it in one day and made him more visible than he had ever been."[6]

In 1991, Clinton officially announced his candidacy for president in the next election and began the fight for the Democratic nomination. By this time he had already demonstrated his resilience and persevering spirit after two failed political campaigns, each of which were followed by significant success. After saving his public image while in the national spotlight during the 1988 election year, it became clear that Clinton had what it took to persevere toward political success. Touting a "New Democrat" message, Clinton billed himself as a refreshing alternative to the traditional Democratic candidates, and by mid-January was enjoying a lead over his strongest competitors for the nomination. However, just weeks before his expected nomination, a tabloid scandal surfaced. A report of an extramarital affair threatened to destroy Clinton's campaign.

Amazingly, with the help of his fiercely loyal wife, Clinton once again overcame seemingly insurmountable odds. He went on to not only capture the Democratic nomination, but also overcame another scandal involving accusations of draft dodging, and ultimately won the election. Clinton's remarkable ability to rebound from setbacks earned him the nickname, "The Comeback Kid." Little did the nation know just how appropriate that moniker would prove to be in the coming years. In reflecting on Clinton's incredible ability to survive adversity, journalist John Harris once said, "Success, misjudgment, in some cases catastrophe, followed by comeback. That resilience is central to who he is as a politician. I think it's central to who he is as a man."[7]

Clinton's lifelong dream was finally realized upon his swearing-in as the forty-second President of the United States, but his troubles were only just beginning. The nation's Capitol was a much different place than the state capitol Clinton had come from, and initially his administration was in a state of near chaos. During his first term, President Clinton fell short of expectations and failed to deliver on many campaign promises—most significantly, national healthcare reform. He also endured more scandal, including suspicion of financial impropriety prior to his presidency, which developed into a drawn-out legal affair that came to be known as "Whitewater."

By the end of his second year in office, Clinton was broadly viewed as a weak and ineffective president, and few expected him to win another term. Once again, he defied expectations. Clinton turned his presidency around in a series of powerful strokes, which included implementing decisive military action to stop the genocide in Bosnia, and withstanding the Republican strong-arm within Congress that forced a government shutdown during federal budget negotiations. He also began to pursue a more moderate path, focusing on winning small legislative victories rather than trying to pass large pieces of legislation that were difficult to get past a Republican-controlled Congress. In 1996, Clinton sailed to victory, winning reelection with more than twice the electoral votes of his opponent, Senator Bob Dole.

Clinton's second term is the one that will most clearly be remembered by history. Halfway through what appeared to be an excellent term, scandal arose once again. Clinton had already weathered more than his share of scandals while in the public eye, but this one was different, because it wasn't about his past indiscretions, it was regarding allegations of sexual misconduct with a White House intern that took place during his presidency. In an ill-conceived attempt to weather yet another storm on the strength of his personality, Clinton ended up getting himself deeper in trouble by lying under oath about the affair. The entire controversy and ensuing impeachment by the House of Representatives would have destroyed a lesser man, but Bill Clinton had a degree of unmatched resilience that saw him through to the end. When a Senate vote failed to convict him, Clinton received yet another second chance.

After successive setback after setback and scandal after scandal, Clinton truly showed his mettle by never giving up. Many people would have conceded the fight in the face of the scathing criticism that President Clinton and his wife faced throughout his administration. But Clinton was not a quitter, and his resilience and uncanny ability to make a comeback and win people over time and time again proved to be one of his very best assets, allowing him the opportunity to keep serving. Betsey Wright, who served as President Clinton's chief of staff, marveled that, "He recovers better than anybody I have ever known. It's extraordinary. I mean he can have horrible things crash down upon his head, but he crawls out from under it and keeps on going."[8] Regardless of personal opinion or political views, one can't deny that Bill Clinton truly is "The Comeback Kid."

13

GEORGE W. BUSH
PRESIDENTIAL LIBRARY & MUSEUM
Dallas, Texas

The drive from my house to the George W. Bush Presidential Center is by far the shortest of all the trips I've made to the presidential libraries and museums across America, but it's no less enjoyable. The neighborhood surrounding Southern Methodist University, where the newest presidential library and museum is located, is simply gorgeous, and I always greatly enjoy the experience of driving through the area and taking in the stately homes and old trees that line the streets.

Thanks to its proximity to my home, I've had the privilege of visiting the presidential center several times since its opening on May 1, 2013, but each time I visit I'm just as impressed as the first. Though less than five miles from downtown Dallas, the library and museum appears to be in its own little Texas oasis, uniquely surrounded by uncut native grasses, colorful wildflowers, and various other indigenous plants and trees. In an unusual contrast to the well-manicured lawns

Twisted piece of steel taken from the wreckage of the World Trade Center

and trimmed hedges usually found at such institutions, the native landscape lends a relaxed, natural feeling to the place. The beautiful yet water-efficient native landscape is just one element of the presidential center that helped it achieve Platinum certification by the U.S. Green Building Council's Leadership in Energy and Environmental Design (LEED) program—a testament to George and Laura Bush's commitment to environmental responsibility and sustainability.[1]

On a recent visit to the library and museum, after parking and approaching the front entrance on foot, I paused for a few minutes to take in the bright sunshine, blue sky, and beautiful white clouds framing the building. The Texas summer wasn't quite in full swing yet, and a light breeze rippled through the tall grass and wildflowers, topping off a gorgeous morning. After getting some great photos of the building and fountain out front, I made my way inside and hurried a step ahead of the crowds to begin my tour.

Having already toured and carefully taken in every exhibit during my previous visits to the museum, this time I focused on my favorite places, beginning with "Responding to September 11." A sobering but powerful gallery of exhibits dedicated to the remembrance of that terrible day and the nation's response, this poignant 9/11 memorial features at its center a giant piece of twisted metal

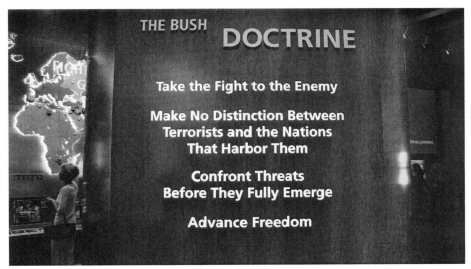

Exhibit featuring President Bush's stance on the War on Terror

taken from the wreckage of the World Trade Center. Around the gallery's outer walls television screens replay news footage from that fateful morning, the images bringing with them a flood of emotions and memories from that day. I vividly remember the shock, grief, and worry; though I was safely at home in Texas, I did not know the whereabouts of my wife, who, as a flight attendant for American Airlines, was in the air at the time. I did not know which flight she was on, and couldn't get through to her for nearly six hours after the attacks began. Thankfully, she was safe, but the hours of not knowing and just wondering and waiting and watching the television felt like an eternity.

Moving on from the difficult but important reminder of how our world changed on that day, my next stop was the Oval Office. Most of the presidential libraries and museums contain some sort of full or partial Oval Office replica, but the George W. Bush museum is the first to allow visitors to walk around inside, examine mementos, and even sit at the desk and have their photo taken within the full-size reproduction of the famous presidential office. Stepping just outside of the Oval Office, I entered the Texas version of the White House Rose Garden, complete with the white colonnade bordering two sides of the garden area. I took several minutes to enjoy the

Replica of Bush's Oval Office, where visitors can have their photo taken

peaceful outdoor setting and take additional photos before heading back inside the museum.

In the next gallery, Life in the White House, I enjoyed the special look inside the walls of America's most famous house, including fun stories of the beloved White House pets, a short video hosted by the Bush twins, Jenna and Barbara, and fascinating questions and answers featuring the White House staff. During my remaining hours in the museum I wound through the exhibits detailing President Bush's major initiatives, policies, and decisions, including the interactive Decision Points Theater that takes participants inside the presidential decision-making process through key events during the Bush administration.

Stepping back into the large lobby area, called Freedom Hall, my eyes were drawn to the top of the sixty-seven-foot structure, where a 360° high-definition video-wall displays an impressive montage of American life and people, reminding visitors of the incredible freedom, diversity, and opportunity that makes America great. Just outside of Freedom Hall there is a courtyard with outdoor seating that services a small coffee shop. In the middle of the courtyard stands a bronze sculpture of former Presidents George W. Bush and George H. W. Bush, father and son standing side by side, facing the

Reproduction of the colonnade adjacent to the White House Rose Garden

building that so artfully preserves the presidential legacy.

As I made my way back through the hall and exited through the gift shop, I reflected on the legacy of America's forty-third president. With his administration so recent and still fresh in the minds and memory of the American people, it will be many years before the full picture of President Bush's legacy is revealed through the lens of history. I am curious how America's future generations will judge his decisions and impact within the context of history. Walking away from the presidential center and back to my car, a quote I had seen inside resonated in my mind as a fitting end to the experience:

> *Now we go forward—grateful for our freedom, faithful to our cause, and confident in the future of the greatest nation on Earth.*[2]

Texas Rose Garden, just outside the Oval Office replica

View of museum from within the Texas Rose Garden

Did You Know?

George W. Bush is the first president to have ever run a marathon. In 1993 he completed the Houston Marathon in 3 hours, 44 minutes, and 52 seconds.

Exhibit depicting life inside the White House

Sculpture of the Bushes' two Scottish Terriers, Barney and Miss Beazley

Did You Know?

While in office, President George W. Bush visited seventy-three countries on official foreign trips.

Exhibit depicting efforts to spread freedom and equality around the world

Gallery titled "Acting With Compassion," showing humanitarian initiatives of the Bush administration

Did You Know?

George and Laura Bush are the first, and so far the only, U.S. President and First Lady to have twins. Their twin daughters, Jenna and Barbara, were born November 25, 1981.

**Display featuring dramatized map representing
the world-wide impact of HIV**

Exhibit detailing the financial crisis during Bush's second term in office

Did You Know?

President Bush was once targeted in a failed assassination attempt in the country of Georgia. On May 10, 2005, a hand grenade was thrown toward the podium where Bush was speaking, but the grenade never detonated. The would-be assassin was later tracked down, arrested, and sentenced to life in prison.

Bronze sculpture of George W. Bush and his father, George H. W. Bush

WHEN YOU VISIT...
DON'T MISS THESE:

- Beautiful natural landscape and Texas wildflowers surrounding the library and museum
- 360° high-definition video shown inside Freedom Hall
- Father and son sculpture inside museum's courtyard
- Responding to September 11 gallery
- Replica of Bush's Oval Office
- Texas Rose Garden
- Life in the White House gallery
- Detailed map of White House interior
- Interactive Decision Points Theater

To see many more photos—in full color—please visit
www.presidentialleadershipbook.com/george-w-bush/photos

"Leadership to me means duty… it means character, and it means listening."

"One of my proudest moments is I didn't sell my soul for the sake of popularity."

"We will not waver; we will not tire; we will not falter, and we will not fail. Peace and freedom will prevail."

GEORGE W. BUSH

Sociable, Assertive, Resolute, and *a Big-Picture Thinker*

FULL NAME: George Walker Bush
LIFESPAN: 67+ years (1946 –)
TERM: 43rd President (R) 2001 – 2009

The presidency of George W. Bush is still fresh in the minds of many Americans, and only history can reveal the true legacy of the Bush administration. Remembered most clearly for his foreign policy decisions following the terrorist attacks of September 11, 2001, Bush united some segments of the nation while alienating others. Regardless of public or personal opinion concerning the policies and decisions of the forty-third U.S. President, it is clear that he demonstrated certain leadership strengths that helped him on his journey to and within the Oval Office.

253

SOCIABLE - able to converse and connect well with others; comfortable and agreeable in company; enjoying the company and interactions of others; friendly, personable, popular.

Sociable leaders genuinely enjoy the company of others and seek opportunities to interact and become involved. Comfortable in crowds or one-on-one, they benefit from the energy of others and enjoy sharing experiences and trading ideas. Sociable leaders encourage discussion and debate, and prefer working with a team over working alone.

George W. Bush was born to parents George H. W. and Barbara Bush years before the senior Bush began to feel the political itch that eventually led him to the presidency. Little "Georgie" Bush came from a long line of distinguished patricians, but his early life was modest, reflecting his parents' desire to shape their future in their own way. The search for independence led the young Bush family to Texas, where son George grew up among his younger siblings in the west Texas town of Midland.

From a very young age, George W. Bush was friendly, outgoing, and a bit of a class clown. His elementary school teacher Austine Crosby recalls young George as a nice and helpful boy who "was always ready to play baseball. He'd round up the other boys and get a game going. He was quite the organizer."[3] Natural leadership ability could be seen early on in young Bush's ability to rally friends together in pursuit of neighborhood adventures and juvenile mischief.

Bush had a knack for connecting with people and was unusually perceptive, even at a young age, which became particularly evident when his little sister, Robin, succumbed to Leukemia shortly before what would have been her fourth birthday. Little Georgie was only seven when his family was suddenly plunged into a period of sobering grief. His father, who was running his own oil company by then, had to continue working and traveling in order to provide for his family, which often left Barbara alone to handle her grief while raising two young sons. Seven-year-old George became extremely close to his mother, taking it upon himself to be her comfort. Years later

Barbara Bush recalled that she had thought she was "being there" for her eldest son, "But," she said, "the truth was he was being there for me."[4]

As he grew up, George W. Bush continued to be friendly, energetic and popular. Friend Clay Johnson once described Bush as being a person whom "People tend to ask to be in charge of the group or be captain of the touch football team. He just has those qualities. People enjoy being around him." Johnson added, "He's very charming. He's not vain at all. He is very interested in the people around him, and people sense that."[5] Being attentive to those around him has always been one of Bush's talents. Yale classmate Michael M. Wood recalls how new pledges to the Delta Kappa Epsilon fraternity were asked to name as many of their fellow recruits as possible. In a room full of about fifty-five Yale freshmen, Bush was the only person present who knew the names of every single one of his fellow pledges.[6] Always an astute observer of people, Bush used this talent to the fullest when he entered the world of politics years later.

The part of politics that Bush really enjoyed the most was working with people; Clay Johnson explained that, "He liked getting out and talking and mixing with small groups and large groups. He just really connected with the crowd... and they connected with him."[7] Another observation from Johnson was that Bush is really good at making fun of himself. Realizing his tendency to stumble over words, Bush has no qualms about having a good laugh at his own expense; "He's the first one who's going to make fun of himself, and it's a very disarming quality."[8]

~◌◌◌~

ASSERTIVE - confident and able to take charge without hesitation; aggressive and decisive in decision-making and in executing plans; self-assured, bold, confident, influential.

Assertive leaders are not afraid to make tough decisions and to take charge in difficult situations. Bold and confident, they don't wait to see what others will do, but instead take initiative to act now. Assertive leaders appreciate action and use their position and influence to get things done quickly.

Longtime *Dallas Morning News* reporter Wayne Slater explains that one defining mark of Bush is his strategy to "only tackle a few things, and tackle them with intensity."[9]   When Bush embarked on his journey into politics—after a false start unsuccessfully campaigning for Congress in 1978—he did so with confidence, gusto and determination. He won his bid for the Texas governorship in 1994, and went on to secure that office for a second term four years later. After that, the next step was the presidency.

When Bush first asked Dick Cheney to be his running mate, Cheney at first declined the invitation. Eventually though, he changed his mind, thanks in part to his realization that George W. Bush was a serious and confident presidential candidate. Bush had determined that if he became president, he was not going to "play it safe." He wanted to get to the Oval Office and make dramatic changes in the areas that he felt needed to be addressed. Ultimately, experienced Washington insider Dick Cheney recognized Bush's drive and potential, and agreed to join the Bush ticket as the vice-presidential candidate. The pair went on to just barely win the 2000 presidential election after a contentious and drawn-out recount that culminated in a Supreme Court ruling and a slim winning margin of just five Electoral College votes.

Bush did not let his narrow win deter him from becoming a strong and assertive president. After being sworn in as the forty-third U.S. President on January 20, 2001, he immediately got down to business, aggressively pursuing his domestic agenda and working to fulfill campaign promises. But as the world clearly remembers, on September 11, 2001 the president's focus suddenly changed. Following the devastating terrorist attacks of that day, the Bush administration vowed to bring to justice the terrorist organization, known as al Qaeda, that was responsible for the attacks. Declaring "War on Terror," President Bush focused much of his administration and his energy on aggressively hunting down and eliminating terrorist activity in the Middle East.

RESOLUTE - firmly resolved in purpose, direction, or opinion; unwavering, determined, focused, steadfast, firm, loyal.

Resolute leaders are firmly decided on a course of action and are not easily deterred from that course. Focused and unwavering, they are determined to accomplish their goal and they will hold fast through adversity and opposition. Resolute leaders are steadfast, reliable, and loyal.

Author Bob Woodward said of Bush, "He is determined to solve problems… Once he is convinced something is a problem, if he has the power to solve it, he will try to solve it."[10] Following the terrorist attacks of 9/11, the rest of Bush's presidency was all but consumed by his desire to solve the problem of terrorism and proactively thwart threats against the security of America. His focused, determined leadership during one of America's greatest times of crisis initially earned him the highest approval rating ever recorded for a U.S. President.[11] However, as time went on, much of the nation—and the world—became disillusioned with Bush's foreign policy decisions. Nonetheless, Bush kept his focus on his target, pursuing what he felt was right and refusing to quail in the face of opposition.

Joe Allbaugh, one of Bush's former campaign managers and aides, explained that Bush is not bashful about his positions, "He doesn't regret decisions that he makes. He wants people to know exactly what he stands for, exactly where he's headed, and exactly where he's coming from, so there'll be no guessing."[12] The question inevitably arises, "Did he make the right decisions?" Obviously no president makes all the right decisions, President Bush included, but ultimately the answer to that question is one that can only be determined by time and perspective. In his book, *Decision Points*, Bush explains:

> *From the beginning, I knew the public reaction to my decisions would be colored by whether there was another attack. If none happened, whatever I did would probably look like an overreaction. If we were*

attacked again, people would demand to know why I hadn't done more. That is the nature of the presidency. Perceptions are shaped by the clarity of hindsight. In the moment of decision, you don't have that advantage.[13]

BIG-PICTURE THINKER - maintaining a broad, overall view of an issue or situation; considerate of long-term outcomes and far-reaching consequences; perceptive, pragmatic.

Shortsighted leaders who focus too narrowly on an issue or situation and fail to consider the big picture very quickly lead themselves and their organizations into trouble. In contrast, big-picture thinkers consistently maintain a broad overall view and are able to perceive and focus on long-term results and consequences. While they cannot predict every possible outcome, leaders who consider the big picture weigh their decisions carefully and value long-term success more than immediate results.

As President of the United States, George W. Bush experienced the constant scrutiny of the press and the public. As he alluded to in his book, *Decision Points*, no matter what decision he chose and what results came of it, Bush came to expect some level of disapproval from someone. Though he was a confident and assertive leader, Bush was also a man who tried to look at every angle before making key decisions. Embracing conservative Christian principles, Bush determined to make decisions that he felt were morally right and served the best interest of his country.

In contrast to his immediate predecessor, President Bush was not a high-achieving student, though he did graduate from Yale and received an MBA from Harvard Business School. Despite his unremarkable academic record, Bush was a very intelligent president with natural political acumen. As president, Bush did not attempt to become an expert on every nuance of the issues he faced, but instead relied upon a trusted circle of knowledgeable and well-educated advisors who presented Bush with the necessary facts to equip him to make well-informed decisions. Through this strategy, Bush demonstrated his commitment to big-picture thinking, revealing that he was a leader who was not afraid to surround himself with people who knew far more about particular subjects than he did. Even so, Bush refused to be spoon-fed ideas, asking countless questions and demanding that his advisors present all the facts and offer different opinions and alternative solutions to each problem.

Above all, in his decision making President Bush sought an answer to the question, "What is the long-term definition of success?" He would get all of his advisors to focus on the long-term goal so that the short-term plans would align with that goal and maximize the probability of making it a reality. Bush realized that short-term, his decisions wouldn't always be popular, but he was focused on the big picture and was willing to take political risks to accomplish what he felt would ultimately result in the best outcome for the most people.

Only history will determine the lasting legacy of President George W. Bush. When author Bob Woodward asked him how he thinks history will remember him, Bush wryly answered, "History? We won't know. We'll all be dead."[14] However history records the legacy of the forty-third U.S. President, it should be remembered that George W. Bush was a leader who did what he felt was right, and who tried his best to provide strong and decisive leadership in a time of fear and uncertainty.

BONUS CHAPTER: 14

ABRAHAM LINCOLN
PRESIDENTIAL LIBRARY & MUSEUM
Springfield, Illinois

Operated by the Illinois Historic Preservation Agency and not affiliated with the U.S. National Archives and Records Administration (NARA) or the NARA's system of presidential libraries and museums.

It was a warm summer day the first time I visited the Abraham Lincoln Presidential Library and Museum in Springfield, Illinois, the city where Lincoln lived and practiced law for more than two decades. Though he did not grow up there, Springfield was the city Abraham Lincoln considered home. In his own words, during his emotional departure for Washington, DC in February 1861, the president elect said, "To this place, and the kindness of these people, I owe everything. Here I have lived a quarter of a century, and have passed from a young man to an old man. Here my children have been born, and one is buried."[1] Sadly, Lincoln was destined to never return to Springfield alive, but it is here that he was laid to rest, along with his wife and children, in the beloved city he called home.

Old State Capitol where Lincoln spent time as a lawyer and politician

It is also in Springfield that the stories and legacy of the sixteenth U.S. President are artfully preserved by the Abraham Lincoln Presidential Library and Museum. The museum and the library archives are housed in two different buildings, separated by Jefferson Street, in the historic downtown section of the city. Just one block southwest of the presidential library is the Old State Capitol, which Lincoln frequented both as a lawyer and as a politician. Across the street from the historic capitol building are the Lincoln-Herndon Law Offices where Lincoln worked for many years prior to becoming president. A few more blocks to the south is the Lincoln Home and visitor center, and Lincoln's Tomb is only a short drive to the northern outskirts of the city.

Upon entering the welcome air conditioning of the museum, I discovered an information desk with a beautifully illustrated wall map depicting the various historic sites in and around Springfield. This large and informative map provides an excellent perspective of the many historic treasures Springfield has to offer. Proceeding down the hallway and past the museum store, I entered a large enclosed plaza that serves as an impressive central hub for the rest of the museum's galleries. In front of me were life-size wax figures of Lincoln and his family, standing in front of the south portico of the White House.

Office where Lincoln practiced law

Leaning against one of the majestic columns of the White House was a wax John Wilkes Booth, ominously staring toward the man he would one day murder. Behind the Lincolns I could see figures of Generals Grant and McClellan standing to one side of the White House entrance, and famous abolitionists Frederick Douglas and Sojourner Truth on the other side.

After marveling over the lifelike wax figures and White House facade, I made my way to the left, where I entered a re-creation of the cabin and surrounding woods where Lincoln grew up in Indiana. Stepping inside the small one-room structure, I carefully studied the cabin's interior, catching a small glimpse of what life was like for a humble frontier family in the 1820s. After spending several minutes inside the modest but fascinating home, I returned to the plaza. Over the course of the next few hours I explored the many other extensive and unique galleries featuring the life and times of Abraham Lincoln and the details of the war that defined his presidency. I was impressed by the meticulous detail, modern technology, and special effects employed in the exhibit designs. A far cry from many traditional museums, the Lincoln Museum draws visitors in—not only to see—but also to touch, feel, hear, and truly experience the story of Abraham Lincoln.

Wax figures of Lincoln family in front of White House facade

By the time I emerged from the museum into the bright August sunlight, my head was spinning with the sights and sounds of nineteenth century America. I had an even greater appreciation for the leadership of Abraham Lincoln, and a much better understanding of some of the most significant events in my nation's history. I walked across the street where I entered the presidential library, previously known as the Illinois State Historical Library. The library houses a premier collection of materials on Illinois history, but is better known as the repository for millions of documents and other archival materials related to the life and presidency of Springfield's most famous resident, Abraham Lincoln. In addition to the extensive archives, the presidential library features occasional exhibits that showcase items from the library's collections. While I was there, I enjoyed the intriguing "Boys in Blue" exhibit, which told the story of Illinois soldiers who served in the Civil War.

The next day I visited the historic Lincoln Home, touring through the very rooms where Abraham and Mary Lincoln lived and raised their family more than 150 years ago. I concluded my tour through history by driving a few miles north to the Oak Ridge Cemetery to pay my respects at Lincoln's final resting place. As I stood in front of the impressive tomb and gazed at the bronze sculpture of Lincoln's

Civil War Generals George B. McClellan and Ulysses S. Grant

head, with its nose shined by the loving and respectful caress of millions of hands, I was filled with a deep sense of patriotism and pride. What a remarkable man and extraordinary legacy. Incredible stories and strong examples like that of Abraham Lincoln are what make me truly proud to be an American!

Did You Know?
Abraham Lincoln was the first Republican to be elected president, the first president to have a beard while in office, and the first president to be assassinated.

Young Abraham Lincoln in front of a re-creation of his boyhood cabin

The Lincoln home in historic Springfield

Did You Know?
Abraham Lincoln kept important notes and letters inside his famous stovepipe hat so that he wouldn't misplace them.

The Lincoln Tomb on outskirts of Springfield

Lincoln sculpture in front of tomb, with nose shined by visitors' hands

Did You Know?

Prior to Abraham Lincoln's assassination by John Wilkes Booth, Booth's brother, Edwin, saved the life of Lincoln's son, Robert, by pulling him to safety when Robert fell into the space between an approaching train and the station platform.

Tombstone marking Lincoln's final resting place

WHEN YOU VISIT...
DON'T MISS THESE:

- Both the presidential museum and the presidential library, located across the street from each other
- The Union Theater featuring the film *Lincoln's Eyes*
- "Ghosts of the Library" special effects presentation
- Journey One gallery: The Pre-Presidential Years
- Journey Two gallery: The White House Years
- "Lying in State," a somber and impactful re-creation of the funeral scene that took place at the Old State Capitol
- Historic Downtown Springfield
- Lincoln-Herndon Law Offices
- Tour of Lincoln home and neighborhood
- Old State Capitol where Lincoln practiced law and gave political speeches
- The Lincoln Tomb, a short drive north of the museum

To see many more photos—in full color—please visit
www.presidentialleadershipbook.com/abraham-lincoln/photos

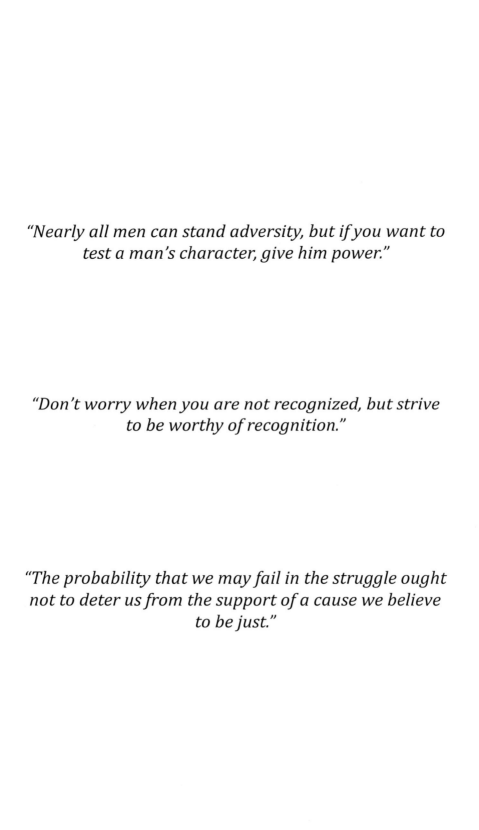

"Nearly all men can stand adversity, but if you want to test a man's character, give him power."

"Don't worry when you are not recognized, but strive to be worthy of recognition."

"The probability that we may fail in the struggle ought not to deter us from the support of a cause we believe to be just."

ABRAHAM LINCOLN
Humble

FULL NAME: Abraham Lincoln
LIFESPAN: 56 years (1809 – 1865)
TERM: 16th President (R) 1861 – 1865

Thousands of books and articles have been written on the life, leadership and wisdom of Abraham Lincoln. There is no question that he is a man greatly admired by Americans and by people around the world. Though more than 150 years have passed since Lincoln was elected the sixteenth President of the United States, he is still consistently ranked by historians and by the American public as the greatest president in the nation's history.[2]

Due to the general familiarity of the public with the life and presidency of Lincoln, and the large amount of material already available regarding this highly esteemed president, I have intentionally chosen not to present a summary of Lincoln's life or a general overview of his many leadership qualities. Instead, I have narrowed my focus to one foundational leadership strength that I feel overwhelmingly permeated Lincoln's life and served as the foundation upon which his other admirable traits were built. That strength is **humility**.

HUMBLE – not arrogant, haughty or conceited; unpretentious and unassuming; modest, courteous, respectful, teachable, selfless.

Humble leaders are able to genuinely relate to and empathize with ordinary people. They don't consider themselves better or more important than others, and are able to easily acknowledge their own shortcomings and laugh at their blunders. Humble leaders realize they don't have all the answers and they are willing to heed the advice and learn from the feedback of others.

Lincoln's humility should not be mistaken for timidity or weakness; he was humble, but confident. While courteous and forbearing, he also possessed an unpretentious demeanor of quiet self-confidence and calm assurance. According to Congressman John B. Alley, a friend of Lincoln's, "In small and unimportant matters, Mr. Lincoln was so yielding that many thought his excessive amiability was born of weakness. But, in matters of vital importance, he was firm as a rock."[3]

Lincoln's confidence was not grounded in his ego, which allowed him to express genuine humility. This combination of gracious humility and firm self-confidence enabled him to be a remarkable servant leader. Historian Doris Kearns Goodwin, who has spent decades studying American presidents and wrote the best-selling book *Team of Rivals: The Political Genius of Abraham Lincoln*, says this about the sixteenth president:

He possessed an uncanny ability to empathize with and think about other people's point of view. He repaired injured feelings that might have escalated into permanent hostility. He shared credit with ease. He assumed responsibility for the failure of his subordinates. He constantly acknowledged his errors and learned from his mistakes. He refused to be provoked by petty grievances. He never submitted to jealousy or brooded over perceived slights.[4]

Each of these remarkable traits that Goodwin has pointed out regarding the leadership of Abraham Lincoln is built upon a solid foundation of humility. In the remainder of this chapter I will take a closer look at these traits and how each reveals the humility that formed the core of President Lincoln's extraordinary leadership.

1. EMPATHIZE WITH OTHERS AND SEE THINGS FROM THEIR POINT OF VIEW

Lincoln did not merely give the appearance of humility. A demeanor of false modesty would not have allowed him to act with such selfless forbearance and to accomplish so much. Lincoln's humility went to his core, and it dated back to his very humble beginnings as a dirt-poor, self-educated frontiersman. He always considered himself a "common man," identifying with ordinary Americans from all walks of life. His early experiences with poverty, loss, and adversity instilled in him a genuine empathy for others. A thoughtful and discerning man, Lincoln had the ability to easily see things from different perspectives and to consider others' points of view.

Lincoln empathized with the common man because he himself was a common man. He had no desire to put on airs or act better than anyone else. Even as Lincoln rose in prominence as an intelligent politician, eloquent orator and quick-witted debater, his easy, humble demeanor did not change. Carl Schurz, a German immigrant who became an avid supporter of Lincoln, recalls his first encounter with the great man:

He talked in so simply and familiar a strain, and his manner and homely phrase were so absolutely free from any semblance of self-consciousness or pretension to superiority, that I soon felt as I had known him all my life and we had long been close friends.[5]

Noah Brooks, a Washington correspondent for the *Sacramento Daily Union* during the Civil War, also wrote of Lincoln's unpretentious demeanor: "No man was ever more free from affectation, and the distaste that he felt for form, ceremony, and personal parade was genuine. Yet he was not without a certain dignity of bearing and character that commanded respect."[6]

Perhaps most notable amongst the examples of Lincoln's empathy toward others is how he treated those most persecuted, feared, or despised. Story upon story is told of Lincoln's kindness and generosity extended toward captured Confederate soldiers, condemned Union Army defectors, and black Americans—both slave and free. Lincoln was known to weep over the injured and fallen Confederate soldiers and to exasperate his generals and secretary of war with his generous granting of pardons for Union Army defectors. Famous black Americans of Lincoln's era such as Frederick Douglas and Sojourner Truth have testified to the kindness and sincerity of Lincoln, which he offered not as a patronizing superior, but simply as a fellow American. Frederick Douglas said of Lincoln, "He was the first great man that I talked with in the United States freely, who in no single instance reminded me of the difference between himself and myself, of the difference of color."[7]

Lincoln's humility and tenderness can also be seen in how he treated children; once, while attending a party in Chicago shortly after his nomination for the presidency, Lincoln was approached by a shy little girl who desired his autograph. The tall guest of honor gave her a smile and, after looking around, said, "But here are other little girls—they will feel badly if I give my name only to you." The child shyly informed him that indeed, there were a total of eight little girls who might like an autograph. Never too important or busy to honor the request of a child, Lincoln proceeded to sit down in the middle of the party and write out a sentence and his name on eight sheets of paper—one for each delighted little girl.[8]

Lincoln's ability to commiserate with others, looking beyond party lines, social classes, racial prejudices, and even the division of the Civil War, made an incredible impact on millions of Americans—young and old, rich and poor, black and white, Union and Confederate.

2. REPAIR INJURED FEELINGS TO PREVENT PERMANENT HOSTILITY

Lincoln, like any man, was not infallible, and would on occasion lose his temper and give vent to his frustrations. However, he invariably would make reparations, dispatching an apology and repairing injured feelings. Lincoln had the strength and humility to apologize for harsh words even when he felt criticism was due, as can be clearly seen in his communications with his generals.

In October 1862, Lincoln sent a short note to General George B. McClellan following an earlier, terse letter in which he had expressed his displeasure at McClellan's failure to pursue the retreating Confederate Army after the battle at Antietam Creek. The note of apology read in part, "Most certainly I intend no injustice to any; and if I have done any, I deeply regret it."[9] On another occasion Lincoln wrote to General Franz Sigel, acknowledging that he may have come across as "a little cross" in an earlier letter, and apologized, saying, "If I was, I ask pardon. If I do get up a little temper I have no sufficient time to keep it up."[10]

Lincoln's ability to lay aside his grievances, acknowledge his faults, and apologize for moments of discourtesy toward others engendered trust, respect, and gratitude in his colleagues and subordinates. His humble and considerate demeanor often ensured that hurt feelings did not escalate into lingering bitterness or animosity that could sabotage critical relationships and undermine his leadership.

3. SHARE CREDIT WITH EASE AND CEDE GLORY TO OTHERS

Lincoln earnestly desired to do something great and memorable for the good of his nation and the world. Not wanting his name to be lost to history, he strove to leave an enduring legacy that would long be remembered and appreciated. As he put it, "Every man is said to have his peculiar ambition. Whether it be true or not, I can say for one that I have no other so great as that of being truly esteemed of my fellow men, by rendering myself worthy of their esteem."[11]

Despite his burning desire to impact the world, Lincoln's humble spirit allowed him to easily put aside his own ego and—not only share credit—but even sacrifice his own welfare and ambition for that of others. Author Henry Ketcham contrasted the humility of Lincoln with the ego of another historic leader, Napoleon Bonaparte:

> *Napoleon was eager to sacrifice the whole of Europe to satisfy the claims of his personal ambition. Lincoln was always ready to stand aside and sacrifice himself for the country. The one was selfishness incarnate; the other was a noble example of a man who never hesitated to subordinate his own welfare to the general good.*[12]

One such example of Lincoln's selflessness can be seen in the story of his 1854 bid for the U.S. Senate. On the first ballot Lincoln took a narrow forty-five to forty-one lead over his pro-slavery opponent, Joel Matteson; however, as the voting proceeded, Lincoln was unable to capture the needed majority to secure his win. Unwilling that the victory be given to a man whose political leanings were so contrary to his own, Lincoln broke the deadlock by withdrawing his candidacy and persuading his supporters to switch their votes to another candidate, Lyman Trumbull, who had received only five votes on the first ballot. For the greater good of his political party, Lincoln preferred Trumbull win the election rather than them both lose to Matteson. Lincoln gave up his lead, threw his support to Trumbull, and ultimately succeeded in giving the victory to the underdog.

By 1856 the Republican Party was beginning to emerge in Illinois politics, and Lincoln, who had previously served four terms as a member of the state legislature, was the most prominent man in the new movement. Lincoln appeared to be the most logical Republican candidate for governor; however, he again put his personal ambition aside for what he felt was the greater good. Refusing to offer his own name for consideration, he instead proposed for nomination Colonel William H. Bissell, a former Democrat who held strong anti-slavery convictions. Lincoln believed Bissell would secure the old Whig vote and enough anti-Nebraska Democrats to win a Republican victory—which he did.

In preparation for a debate with incumbent Senator Stephen Douglas during the 1858 senatorial race, Lincoln chose, despite the urgings of his friends, to pose a question about the controversial topic of slavery in the U.S. territories. If Douglas answered the question one way, it would alienate his Illinois constituents, but if he answered the other way, it would alienate southern Democrats. Lincoln knew as well as his friends that asking the question would likely cost Lincoln the senatorial race, however, he explained, "Gentlemen, I am killing larger game. If Douglas answers, he can never be president, and the battle of 1860 is worth a hundred of this."[13] As author Henry Ketcham explains, it's unlikely that Lincoln expected at that time to be a contender in the 1860 presidential election, but he saw the danger of Douglas becoming president, and "he was willing to surrender the senatorial election to save the country from a Douglas administration."[14] On the day of the debate, Lincoln asked the question. Douglas's answer infuriated southern Democrats and endeared his Illinois constituents, and while the question did cost Lincoln the senatorship, the answer cost Douglas the presidency two years later.

Lincoln's humble willingness to put aside his ego and share the spotlight is most evident in his selection of his cabinet after being elected to the presidency. Contrary to popular practice, Lincoln did not draw his cabinet selections exclusively from friends, political allies, and those to whom he owed a favor. Instead, his diverse cabinet included many of Lincoln's former rivals for political office. Lincoln explained: "I need them all. They enjoy the confidence of their several states and sections, and they will strengthen the administration. The times are too grave and perilous for ambitious schemes and rivalries."[15]

Lincoln went on to say, "Let us forget ourselves and join hands, like brothers, to save the republic. If we succeed, there will be glory enough for us all."[16] While Lincoln firmly established his authority and leadership as president, he did not hesitate to take the council of his former rivals and to share credit with every member of his administration.

4. ASSUME RESPONSIBILITY FOR THE FAILURE OF SUBORDINATES

President Lincoln did not hesitate to assume responsibility for mistakes and failings of his subordinates. In his book *Lincoln On Leadership*, author Donald T. Phillips states that Lincoln "readily accepted responsibility for the battles lost during the Civil War. He tried to let his generals know that if they failed, he too failed."[17] Lincoln was humble enough to refrain from pointing fingers or assigning blame, and instead acknowledged his burden of responsibility as the nation's highest executive.

On one such occasion, public ire was kindled toward Union General George B. McClellan when he failed to provide adequate support to Field Commander John Pope during the unsuccessful second battle of Bull Run. David T. Phillips explains, "It was generally believed at the time that McClellan wanted Pope to fail. As a result, several angered cabinet officers signed a letter of protest condemning McClellan for his conduct during the battle and demanded his dismissal."[18] President Lincoln disagreed and chose to stand behind his general. Disregarding the demand for his dismissal, he instead appointed him to even greater responsibility. Upon learning of the appointment,

An infuriated Secretary of War Stanton exclaimed that no such order had been issued from the War Department. Lincoln then responded

somewhat calmly, "No, Mr. Secretary, the order was mine; and I will be responsible for it to the country." Lincoln felt that McClellan should not have to bear the entire burden for the loss. He also felt that there were no other officers who were better suited to the command.[19]

On another occasion, when the incompetence of Lincoln's first Secretary of War, Simon Cameron, became apparent and Cameron faced the censure of Congress, Lincoln publicly took the blame. Historian Doris Kearns Goodwin explains, "If fault was to be found, then he himself and his entire Cabinet 'were at least equally responsible.' For this, Cameron would be forever grateful."[20]

Time and again Lincoln humbly put his own reputation on the line as he stood behind his subordinates, at times defending their decisions or actions, and at times publicly taking the blame for their mistakes or failures. His sense of personal responsibility and accountability earned him respect and trust, and his loyalty to those whom he led earned him, in turn, their loyalty and admiration.

5. ACKNOWLEDGE ERRORS AND LEARN FROM MISTAKES

Lincoln was a confident leader, but he was not over-confident; he knew that he was fallible. As such, he had the humility and courage to admit when he was wrong and to make amends. He was also committed to never stop learning—he did not assume to be an expert on any particular subject, and readily accepted the wisdom of others. One of Lincoln's closest friends, Joshua Speed, said of Lincoln, "When he was ignorant on any subject, no matter how simple it might make him appear, he was always willing to acknowledge it."[21] Congressman John B. Alley, also a friend of Lincoln's, stated, "Of all these public men, none seemed to have so little pride of opinion. He was always learning and did not adhere to views which he found to be erroneous, simply because he had once formed and held them."[22]

During the long and bloody Civil War that encompassed almost the entirety of Lincoln's presidency, the wearied Commander in Chief endured much frustration and disappointment when dealing with his generals. Though his military background was limited to his short tenure as a volunteer in the Black Hawk War, as president Lincoln developed a keen understanding of military strategy. Because of this, he was able to make perceptive judgments regarding the strategy and decisions of his military leaders. Even so, Lincoln's judgments were not always accurate, and when he discovered so, he readily acknowledged his error. One such example can be seen in an excerpt from a letter he wrote to General Ulysses S. Grant, dated July 13, 1863:

> *I never had any faith, except a general hope that you knew better than I, that the Yazoo Pass expedition and the like could succeed. When you got below and took Port Gibson, Grand Gulf, and vicinity, I thought you should go down the river and join General Banks, and when you turned northward, east of the Big Black, I feared it was a mistake. I now wish to make the personal acknowledgment that you were right and I was wrong.*[23]

Lincoln's willingness to humble himself and acknowledge and learn from his mistakes resonated with those whom he led. To receive an apology from and to be encouraged and affirmed by their leader—the President of the United States—undoubtedly stirred in Lincoln's subordinates pride, dedication, and even greater determination to serve wholeheartedly.

⟨∘✻∘⟩

6. REFUSE TO BE PROVOKED BY PETTY GRIEVANCES

Leonard Swett, a lawyer and political ally of Lincoln's, once described Lincoln as "a very poor hater." Indeed, though Lincoln could be angered, annoyed or frustrated like any man, he very rarely developed deep resentment or held grudges. Swett went

on to say of Lincoln,

> *He never judged men by his like or dislike for them. If any given act was to be performed, he could understand that his enemy could do it just as well as anyone. If a man had maligned him, or been guilty of personal ill-treatment and abuse, and was the fittest man for the place, he would put him in his cabinet just as soon as he would his friend. I do not think he ever removed a man because he was his enemy, or because he disliked him.*[24]

Lincoln received more than his fair share of insults and snubs during his lifetime, and particularly in his political career. While he was not callous to these abuses, his humble, gentle spirit enabled him to shrug off offenses and grievances that a lesser man could not have ignored.

On one occasion, President Lincoln called upon General George B. McClellan at his home, only to find that the general had not yet returned from attending a wedding. After Lincoln had patiently waited for about an hour, General McClellan returned, only to pass by the president without a word on his way to his bedroom. Another thirty minutes passed before the president and his party were informed by a servant that the general had gone to bed. Those accompanying Lincoln were outraged, but the president quietly said that it was "better at this time not to be making points of etiquette & personal dignity."[25]

Lincoln's distinct ability to overlook such offenses and not let his leadership be dictated by a bruised ego set him apart from his colleagues. He did not allow himself to be walked on, but he did choose his battles with great care; as he put it, "No man resolved to make the most of himself has time to waste on personal contention."[26]

7. NEVER SUBMIT TO JEALOUSY OR BROOD OVER PERCEIVED SLIGHTS

L incoln was confident in his own abilities and did not foster any insecurity that would lead him to feel threatened by or jealous of others. As author Donald T. Phillips puts it in his book, *Lincoln on Leadership*, Lincoln "had faith and confidence in himself and didn't need ego-stroking or constant reinforcement."[27] This confidence, coupled with his remarkable humility, enabled Lincoln to handle unjust criticism, slander, libel and hatred with patience and determination, and without becoming defensive or retaliatory. This is not to say that Lincoln never defended himself or argued in opposition to public opinion or belief—indeed, he was very well-practiced in defending his position and pursuing an unpopular agenda. However, even his most vehement argument or defense was done so not in hotheaded emotion, but in a careful, courteous and logical manner.

Often, to avoid responding in anger, Lincoln would deal with harsh criticism and other frustrations by writing out a letter refuting the criticism or offense, and then file the letter away, never to be sent. This habit bears witness to Lincoln's human sensitivity, while also demonstrating his judicious and mature handling of his emotions. Lincoln was indeed affected and even hurt by the verbal attacks he so often received while in office, yet he had the strength, courage, and humility to not respond in kind.

In November 1862 President Lincoln made the difficult decision to relieve General George B. McClellan of command over the Union forces. Less than two years later, during Lincoln's 1864 bid for reelection, his Democratic opponent was none other than General McClellan. McClellan, still angry over his dismissal, became a bitter rival and serious contender for the presidency. In the midst of the campaign, Lincoln learned that a Union Army officer had been relieved of his command due to his support of McClellan's candidacy. Lincoln, with his characteristic humility, lack of jealousy, and self-deprecating humor, immediately ordered the officer's reinstatement, saying, "Supporting General McClellan for the presidency is no violation of army regulations, and as a question of taste in choosing between him and me—well, I'm the longest, but he's better looking."[28]

Without a doubt, the genuine, gracious humility of Abraham Lincoln served him exceedingly well as a leader. Always understanding, always forgiving, always willing to learn and to serve, it is no surprise that Lincoln is considered by so many to be the greatest president in America's history. One of Lincoln's contemporaries, John H. Littlefield, a law student who studied in Lincoln's Springfield law office for a time, described this great man as modest in demeanor, yet as conveying an impression of strong individuality. Littlefield said of Lincoln, "I never in all my life associated with a man who seemed so ready to serve another."[29] It was this attitude of humble servant leadership that enabled this man to reach such remarkable heights of achievement, and that put the name Abraham Lincoln in the history books forever.

CALL TO ACTION

Based on the leadership strengths featured and explained in this book, I urge you to create and immediately apply

A SUCCESS SYSTEM THAT NEVER FAILS

I hope you have enjoyed the journey through the life and times of these former U.S. Presidents and have gained new insights into their leadership and into your potential to significantly improve your own leadership strengths. I also hope that you have been encouraged to personally visit and experience these national treasures known as the United States Presidential Libraries and Museums. However, I strongly suggest that you don't just read and enjoy this book and then set it back on the shelf and be done with it. I encourage you to be focused and intentional in using this book to improve your leadership by applying these proven strengths, and thus achieve greater success!

If you've come this far, there's no doubt you have realized the important role these leadership strengths played in the lives, accomplishments and legacies of these American presidents. It's my firm belief that focusing on and improving your strengths will bring you far greater success than fixating on and worrying about your weaknesses.

Without question, everyone has unique strengths and weaknesses. Of the forty-seven impactful leadership strengths featured in this book, many no doubt align with your own leadership strengths. I urge you to identify and select three high-priority strengths for immediate focus on improvement. Specifically, three strengths you believe will have the most positive impact on your leadership and your life. For a full list of the leadership strengths featured in this book, please refer to the Index on page 315.

Form Good Habits and Become Their Slave

In the mid-1700s Benjamin Franklin developed a personal system for cultivating his character by focusing on improving in thirteen areas, or virtues. After selecting and defining each virtue, Franklin charted them out in a little book, which he kept with him at all times. He devoted one week at a time to each virtue, committing on a daily basis to focus on practicing that particular virtue through-out the day. At the end of each day, he would spend a few minutes honestly reflecting on whether or not he had truly adhered to that week's selected virtue. If upon reflection he found some fault in his behavior that day in respect to that goal, he would mark a small dot for that day on the chart in his book. He continued this process, day-by-day, week-by-week, for thirteen weeks, then began again, with the goal of decreasing the number of dots marked in his book until he could complete each week without adding any dots.[1]

Similar to Benjamin Franklin's personal mission to improve his character through very intentional focus and repetition, there is a story written by Og Mandino of a youth who strove to become the greatest salesman in the world. He accomplished his goal through careful study and intentional repetition of important principles written in a series of ten scrolls. Beginning with the first scroll, the young man committed to read through the entire scroll once in the morning, once at noon, and once in the evening for thirty consecu-tive days. Afterwards he moved on to the second scroll and repeated the same process, then the third scroll, and so on until after 300 days he had completed the process with all ten scrolls.[2]

Through their individual methods, both Benjamin Franklin and the youth in Og Mandino's story were absolutely committed to their personal goals of forming new, good habits through intentional repetition and practice. In an excerpt from Og Mandino's *The Greatest Salesman in the World*, the power and impact of habits is explained:

> *In truth, the only difference between those who have failed and those who have succeeded lies in the difference of their habits. Good habits are the key to all success. Bad habits are the unlocked door to failure.*

Thus, the first law I will obey, which precedeth all others is—I will form good habits and become their slave.[3]

There lies the key to any success system—forming good habits and "becoming their slave." The two systems mentioned above, whether implemented through charts and dots or by repeated readings three times a day, are both ways of forming and ingraining new habits. Similar to the concept of spaced learning, this careful and intentional repetition over an extended period of time is one of the most effective ways to absorb and internalize information and improve behavior and habits. Rather than try to accomplish something all at once or spend one extended period of time focusing on a task, it is far better to spend a shorter amount of time on it, take a break, and then return your focus to it again. Repeating this process over the course of the day, week, month, or year (depending on your goals) undoubtedly will produce the results you desire and enable you to become more effective and successful.

Commit to and Apply a Success System That Never Fails

You may feel the two examples above are excellent and practical, or you may consider them to be rather laborious and extreme. Either way, I cannot over-emphasize the critical importance of developing and implementing a success system that works for you. A well-planned system of spaced learning and focused, intentional repetition, if followed seriously and consistently, will not fail.

The bottom line is that you must be intentional in identifying and selecting the very few most important leadership strengths that will have the most dramatic and positive impact in your life and leadership. Then implement a strategy and commit to focusing on and refining those strengths in the coming weeks, months, and years. Without question, the result will be achieving greater personal, professional, and organizational success in your life!

Knowing that everyone learns differently and one-size does not fit all, I intentionally have chosen not to outline here a specific method for you to follow. However, I have provided some tips, suggestions, and general principles that I believe you will find helpful in creating and consistently applying your own *Success System that Never Fails.*

Consider These Tips, Strategies and Suggestions

- **PUT IT IN WRITING.** It's easy to get excited about setting out toward achieving an important goal, but maintaining enthusiasm, focus, and commitment over time is much more difficult. You will dramatically help yourself achieve clarity and maintain focus and inspiration by putting your specific goals, in this case improving specific leadership strengths, in writing. It is crucial that you write a crystal clear, action-oriented definition of what maximum success, relative to that leadership strength, will look like, feel like, and what it will accomplish. In other words, clearly and precisely define true success for you relative to each leadership strength you select to focus on and improve. Also, put in writing the many positive rewards and benefits that will accrue to you and those around you as you improve and daily demonstrate improved leadership strengths. It is also important to carefully think through and put in writing specifically how you intend to pursue your goal. Then, be sure to put what you have written in several places where you will see and can review daily. For example, you might put a copy of your personal *Success System That Never Fails* on your mobile device, your desk, your bathroom counter, your bedside table, and even on a frequently used mirror.
- **MAKE IT SIMPLE AND ACCESSIBLE.** Whether you create something as simple as a manual system—using a pen or pencil and an index card or small book—or a digital system loaded on your computer or mobile device, it is absolutely crucial that the system be very simple, very easy to track and monitor, and very easy to carry with you at all times. Morning, noon and evening, this simple success system should always be easily accessible. Frequently and consistently reviewing it is the key to effective application and follow-through.
- **START SMALL.** Don't try to focus on several strengths at once; if spread too thin, you will make little progress. Instead, in order

to truly be effective, you must start small and be very focused and disciplined. Select only the very few (I suggest no more than three) most important and appropriate leadership strengths that will make the greatest positive impact in your life and in the lives of those you lead. After reaching your goal of improving those first few strengths, you can then shift your focus to another two or three strengths and begin the process anew.

- **TAKE IT ONE WEEK AT A TIME.** I recommend that you follow the example of Benjamin Franklin and focus on just one of the leadership strengths you have selected for an entire week. One week is not long, but by applying singular focus on that leadership strength each day for one week, you will begin to see results. The following week, focus on the second leadership strength you've chosen, then the third, etc. Once you've spent one week on each of the three leadership strengths you have selected, start again with the first. By limiting yourself to one week at a time, you will maintain focus and discipline that could fade if attempted over a longer period of time. Repeat this three-week process over and over until you have ingrained, internalized and maximized improvement in each of the crucial leadership strengths you have selected.

- **REVIEW DAILY.** Be very intentional every day to review and reflect on the leadership strength you have chosen to focus on. Ideally, do so three times—in the morning, midday, and in the late afternoon or evening. Don't merely think about the leadership strength you have chosen, but instead ask yourself, "Specifically, within the past twenty-four hours what did I do or not do to exhibit and model leadership excellence in the area I have chosen? What can I do today and tomorrow to more effectively and consistently exhibit leadership excellence relative to the strength on which I am focused?" It is critically important that you take the time and make the effort to be very specific as you honestly reflect on and answer these questions and seek ways to improve.

- **APPLY SPACED LEARNING.** Regardless of the issue, skill, or practice in any area of your life, you virtually never reach your potential in one sitting or session. It takes concentrated, consistent practice and refinement over a period of time. That is the essence and power of spaced learning. Whether you desire to memorize an inspirational poem, learn to play an instrument, change a well-ingrained habit or create a new one, it is almost always necessary to engage in consistent spaced learning. New habits, new skills, new attitudes, and new behaviors demand consistent spaced learning, and the same is true in improving your leadership habits, skills, attitudes and behaviors. A high-impact leadership strength must be learned and carefully refined and ingrained into a strong behavior and habit over time. Commit to taking the time necessary to do so through spaced learning.

- **BE ACCOUNTABLE.** Create a small group made up of highly trusted friends and colleagues with whom you can share your goals for focusing on and improving your leadership strengths. Frequently ask these friends and colleagues for honest feedback on your progress. Better yet, encourage them to also study the book and work on improving leadership strengths most appropriate for each of them. Then commit to support, help and encourage each other to remain inspired and accountable to the goals each has selected.

- **TEACH OTHERS.** One of the most powerful and enduring ways to refine, ingrain and solidify new habits, new skills, new attitudes and new behaviors is to teach and mentor others. Throughout my life, in various formal and informal teaching roles, I have found it true over and over that "the teacher learns more than the student." As you advance toward your personal goal of refining and improving the leadership strengths you've selected, find ways to model and teach those strengths to those whom you lead and influence. I guarantee—you both will benefit!

- **ENGAGE YOUR TEAM.** Use this book as a key resource to lead your team or direct reports in a focused effort to improve upon selected leadership strengths. Joining together and creating accountability within a highly effective leadership improvement network is an excellent way to achieve greater success both personally and professionally.

- **SCHEDULE AN INSPIRATIONAL PRESENTATION.** Consider kicking off a team meeting, leadership retreat, or an annual or special meeting with my Presidential Leadership presentation or extended workshop. Whether it's facilitating a small team discussion or speaking at a large organization or association meeting, I will customize this presentation to best meet your needs. If you are interested in using this book as a resource in a group setting, special bulk pricing may be available. To find out more information about my speaking availability or about bulk book pricing, please contact me via my website, www.dannielsen.com.

The key to your personal *Success System That Never Fails* is commitment, simplicity and consistency. By making your success strategy simple to understand, follow, access, and measure progress, you can commit to putting it into practice on a daily basis for the next year, five years, or even the rest of your life. With your *Success System That Never Fails,* you can apply these strengths, develop leadership excellence, and achieve greater personal, professional and organizational success!

Acknowledgments

This book would not have happened without the contributions of the wonderful people listed below. From the bottom of my heart, thank you.

– Dan Nielsen

Faye Nielsen

Thank you to my wife Faye, who is truly one of the world's very special ladies. In addition to serving as a flight attendant with American Airlines, Faye is a talented and successful interior designer. Not only does she create beautiful, functional spaces for her clients, she also creates and shares trust, loyalty, joy, and love. Many of Faye's clients become close personals friends—a testament to the truth that actions speak far louder than words. Simply put, people want to be around talented, uplifting, positive and accepting people like my wonderful wife, Faye Nielsen.

Faye puts up with me—well, most of the time! She understands and patiently supports my personal and professional drive, curiosity and life-long love for learning, writing, presenting, traveling America the Beautiful, photography, history and leadership. For her love, understanding, and support I am eternally grateful.

Staff and Volunteers of the Presidential Libraries and Museums

I would like to take special note of the immeasurable contribution of the thousands of wonderful people who have dedicated countless hours to the creation and operation of the United States Presidential Libraries and Museums. These incredible people are committed to serving every visitor who walks in the doors for a look inside the life and times of a former U.S. President.

Through their painstaking preparations and by graciously providing guidance and answering questions, these staff and volunteers truly enhance the experience at each library and museum, and without them this book never would have happened.

EMILY SIRKEL

My coauthor, Emily, is an outstanding young lady. She represents the very best of a generation that will soon lead America and the world, and I have been honored to partner with her in writing this book on leadership.

I am a man of faith. There is absolutely no question in my mind that meeting Emily on a cold December day in 2011 at "my Starbucks" was providential. The unlikely, but true, story of how we met reinforces my belief that our meeting was not merely by chance. Thanks to God's providence and the allure of hot coffee on a cold day, we began this journey together, pursuing the unique and priceless opportunity to work together as a team in order to better serve others.

Emily is an excellent and organized (oh, do I need that!) writer and researcher. She is a superb example of a true team player and exemplifies the power of teamwork. Even though her total personal and professional life experiences are one-third of mine, she consistently demonstrates greater talents, skills, abilities and potential in many areas than I do.

Though she has many talents, by far Emily's greatest strength and asset is her personal integrity. Through her diligence and integrity she has earned my confidence, and I trust her implicitly, which she never takes for granted. Trust is crucial for teamwork and leadership excellence, and it's that trust that makes our partnership so valuable.

Thank you Emily for coming into my life—becoming not just an employee, but my partner. Thank you for working with me in order to better serve others in their quest to create greater value, become better leaders, and thereby achieve greater success.

By myself, this book would have never been written. So with

the utmost gratitude I thank Emily for her commitment, consistency and many contributions—without her this book would not exist. By following my instincts, and not just hiring, but partnering with this remarkable young lady, the completed book is now in your hands. And that, my colleagues and friends, is the essence of effective teamwork and leadership!

OTHER KEY CONTRIBUTORS

The creation of this book has been a lengthy, but rewarding, process. Throughout the weeks, months and years of traveling, planning, researching, writing, and editing there have been a number of people who have generously offered assistance, support, and encouragement along the way. From the honest advice of trusted colleagues, to the faithful support of close friends and family, to the enthusiastic interest of complete strangers—I greatly cherish and appreciate the help I've received along the way.

I would like to extend special thanks to my daughter, Christi Nielsen, and my longtime friend and colleague, Harla Adams, who have both contributed their time and expertise to assist in the proofreading and editing process. Your assistance and thoughtful comments are greatly appreciated.

About the Authors

Dan **Nielsen** is a successful leader, entrepreneur, teacher, author and speaker. A perpetual student, Dan understands the incredible power of learning from successful leaders and strongly believes that leadership excellence is the key to all lasting progress and success.

Dan spent much of his career as a healthcare executive, serving for fifteen years as the President and CEO of Dallas-Ft. Worth Medical Center, and nearly fifteen years as the lead executive responsible for the national education and networking strategies and activities of VHA, America's largest hospital and healthcare national alliance.

Dan is now a leader, speaker, and author with a much broader area of interest than just healthcare. He is passionate about helping others reach their potential and achieve greater success, no matter who you are or how you define it. He regularly writes and speaks about achieving greater success, becoming a better leader, and living an inspired and joy-filled life. To see more of Dan's writing and to learn about his dynamic, inspirational presentations, please visit his website at www.dannielsen.com, and look on page 298 to see a description of his top three presentations.

Whenever he gets a chance, Dan continues to pursue two of his favorite hobbies—travel and photography. When not at home or out traveling across America the Beautiful in his motorhome, which he fondly calls his "Inspirational Vehicle," Dan can usually be found getting some work done either in his favorite chair at Starbucks or while walking at the gym. Dan has two grown children and two grandchildren and lives near Dallas, Texas with his wife, Faye.

—⌒✦⌒—

Emily Sirkel is a writer with a talent for providing written structure for Dan's vision, taking his big ideas and putting them into written form. Emily has worked with Dan since the beginning of 2012, serving as his coauthor, researcher, editor, collaborator, content developer, web admin, and "unrelenting taskmaster" on a full-time basis.

Emily has a bachelor's degree completely unrelated to writing, and a unique background that includes diverse experiences such as being a homeschooled ranch-kid in eastern Montana and a camp food service director in central Texas. Despite her patchwork résumé, Emily has a talent and passion for communicating, especially in written form. She has been addicted to books since her mom taught her to read at the age of four, and she developed a love for writing soon after that.

In addition to the writing she does with Dan, she pursues her other writing interests on her website, www.emilysirkel.com. Emily and her husband, Geoff, live near Dallas, Texas, where they are actively involved in church and are eagerly anticipating the arrival of their first child in November 2013.

—⌒✦⌒—

PRESENTATIONS

BY DAN NIELSEN

PRESIDENTIAL LEADERSHIP
Learning from United States Presidential Libraries & Museums

The United States Presidential Libraries & Museums offer a rare 'backstage pass' that takes visitors behind the scenes of the life and leadership of America's former presidents. I am privileged to be one of very few people in the world who has personally visited, studied and extensively photographed each of these storehouses of American history. Through this experience, I have identified highly relevant and effective leadership strengths demonstrated by each of fourteen U.S. Presidents whose legacies are preserved by these fascinating institutions. In this presentation I share and illustrate these important leadership strengths along with exclusive photos I've taken at each library and museum. No matter political preference, participants will enjoy this unique and uplifting presentation while learning from the strengths of some of the world's most prestigious and powerful former leaders.

To learn more, please visit:
www.dannielsen.com/speaking/presidential-leadership

Sharpen Your Focus
Achieving Clarity for More Effective Leadership

In this increasingly chaotic and demanding world, effective, focused leadership has never been more difficult or crucial. As a leader, you must continuously sharpen your focus in order to achieve greater clarity for precise and strategic leadership. In a refreshing break from the ordinary, I provide proven strategies for achieving and communicating greater clarity, illustrating each concept through powerful imagery that features my personal photography throughout America the Beautiful.

To learn more, please visit:

www.dannielsen.com/speaking/sharpen-your-focus

Strategies for Greater Success
Achieving Your Highest Priorities
& Reaching Your Full Potential

As a fervent believer in life-long learning, I am constantly seeking the best wisdom and insights from world-class leaders and achievers. Through this process, I have identified key strategies that are essential for achieving greater success in life and business. In this presentation I share these proven, actionable strategies, explaining why they are essential and illustrating each with meaningful, memorable examples.

To learn more, please visit:

www.dannielsen.com/speaking/strategies-for-greater-success

Resources
For Further Study

Iencourage you to visit and utilize my specially designed resource website, **www.presidentialleadershipbook.com**, where you will find interesting facts, powerful quotes, useful links, hundreds of full-color photographs, and much more. I have also provided below a selection of other websites that I found to be the most informative and reliable during my research, and I encourage you to utilize these online resources for further information on the lives, leadership, and impact of the United States Presidents:

- The presidential libraries webpage of the NARA: **http://www.archives.gov/presidential-libraries/about/**
- The website of the Herbert Hoover Presidential Library and Museum: **http://hoover.archives.gov**
- The website of the Herbert Hoover Presidential Library Association: **http://www.hooverassociation.org/index.php**
- The website of the Franklin D. Roosevelt Presidential Library and Museum: **http://www.fdrlibrary.marist.edu**
- The website of the Harry S. Truman Presidential Library and Museum: **http://www.trumanlibrary.org**
- The website of the Dwight D. Eisenhower Presidential Library and Museum: **http://www.eisenhower.archives.gov**
- The website of the John F. Kennedy Presidential Library and Museum: **http://www.jfklibrary.org**
- The website of the Lyndon B. Johnson Presidential Library and Museum: **http://www.lbjlibrary.org**
- The website of the Richard Nixon Presidential Library and Museum: **http://www.nixonlibrary.gov**

- The website of the Gerald R. Ford Presidential Library and Museum: **http://www.fordlibrarymuseum.gov**
- The website of the Gerald R. Ford Presidential Foundation: **http://www.geraldrfordfoundation.org**
- The website of the Jimmy Carter Presidential Library and Museum: **http://www.jimmycarterlibrary.gov**
- The website of the Carter Center: **http://www.cartercenter.org/index.html**
- The website of the Ronald Reagan Presidential Library and Museum: **http://www.reaganfoundation.org**
- The website of the George Bush Presidential Library and Museum: **http://bushlibrary.tamu.edu**
- The website of the William J. Clinton Presidential Library and Museum: **http://www.clintonlibrary.gov**
- The website of the William J. Clinton Presidential Center: **http://www.clintonpresidentialcenter.org**
- The website of the George W. Bush Presidential Library and Museum: **http://www.georgewbushlibrary.smu.edu**
- The website of the George W. Bush Presidential Center: **http://www.bushcenter.org**
- The website of the Abraham Lincoln Presidential Library and Museum: **http://alplm.org**
- The website of the White House: **http://www.whitehouse.gov**
- The website of the U.S. Senate: **http://www.senate.gov**
- The website of the U.S. Army Center of Military History: **http://www.history.army.mil**
- The website of the Miller Center: **http://millercenter.org**
- The website of the Hauenstein Center for Presidential & Leadership Studies: **http://hauensteincenter.org**
- The website of the Public Broadcasting Service (PBS): **http://www.pbs.org**
- The website of the Cable-Satellite Public Affairs Network (C-SPAN): **http://www.c-span.org**

For a more detailed listing of the individual sources used during my research, please consult the Notes on page 302

Notes

Introduction

1.   "Presidential Library History," U.S. National Archives website, accessed March 28, 2013, http://www.archives.gov/presidential-libraries/about/history.html.

Chapter 1 – Herbert Hoover

1.   Herbert Hoover, as quoted and displayed in the Herbert Hoover Presidential Library and Museum, viewed July 22, 2011.

2.   Cynthia Haven, "How the U.S. saved a starving Soviet Russia," *Stanford News*, April 4, 2011, http://news.stanford.edu/news/2011/april/famine-040411.html.

3.   Herbert Hoover, as quoted in "Herbert Hoover," the website of the White House, accessed March 13, 2013, http://www.whitehouse.gov/about/presidents/herberthoover.

4.   Lou Henry Hoover, in letter to Herbert and Allan Hoover, July 1932, viewed on C-SPAN website, March 13, 2013, http://presidentiallibraries.c-span.org/Content/Hoover/For_Herbert.pdf.

5.   D. Elton Trueblood, as quoted and displayed in the Herbert Hoover Presidential Library and Museum, viewed July 22, 2011.

Chapter 2 – Franklin D. Roosevelt

1.   Franklin D. Roosevelt, address to Congress requesting a declaration of war, December 8, 1941, viewed on Miller Center website, March 15, 2013, http://millercenter.org/president/speeches/detail/3324.

2.   Franklin D. Roosevelt, first inaugural address, March 4, 1933, viewed on Miller Center website, March 15, 2013, http://millercenter.org/president/speeches/detail/3280.

3. Franklin D. Roosevelt, address to Democratic National Convention following his nomination for the presidency, July 2, 1932, viewed on TeachingAmericanHistory.org, March 15, 2013, http://teachingamericanhistory.org/library/document/acceptance-speech-at-the-democratic-convention/.

4. Franklin D. Roosevelt, address to graduating class at Oglethorpe University, May 22, 1932, viewed on the New Deal Network website, March 15, 2013, http://newdeal.feri.org/speeches/1932d.htm.

5. Eleanor Roosevelt, as quoted in "American President: Franklin Delano Roosevelt—A Life In Brief," Miller Center website, accessed March 14, 2013, http://millercenter.org/president/fdroosevelt/essays/biography/.

Chapter 3 – Harry Truman

1. Harry S. Truman, as said to a reporter c. 1944, quoted in "Harry S. Truman, 34th Vice President (1945)," on the website of the United States Senate, accessed March 13, 2013, http://www.senate.gov/artandhistory/history/common/generic/VP_Harry_Truman.htm.

2. Eleanor Roosevelt, as reportedly said to Harry S. Truman following the death of Franklin D. Roosevelt, April 12, 1945.

3. Harry S. Truman, as said in remarks to reporters, April 13, 1945, quoted and displayed by the Harry S. Truman Presidential Library and Museum, viewed July 21, 2011.

4. "Historians Presidential Leadership Survey: Overall Ranking," C-SPAN, 2000-2009, http://legacy.c-span.org/PresidentialSurvey/Overall-Ranking.aspx.

5. "Historians Presidential Leadership Survey: Pursued Equal Justice for All," C-SPAN, 2000-2009, http://legacy.c-span.org/PresidentialSurvey/Pursued-Equal-Justice-For-All.aspx.

6. Harry S. Truman, remarks during address to crowd in Sandusky, Ohio, October 26, 1948, quoted and displayed by the Harry S. Truman Presidential Library and Museum, viewed July 21, 2011.

Chapter 4 – Dwight Eisenhower

1. Dialogue as related by Dwight D. Eisenhower, *At Ease: Stories I Tell to Friends* (Garden City: Doubleday & Company, 1967), 18.

2.   Dwight D. Eisenhower to James Hagerty on way to press conference, March 23, 1955, as related by Fred L. Greenstein during interview that appeared in the documentary, *WGBH American Experience: Eisenhower*, produced by PBS, 1993, http://www.pbs.org/wgbh/americanexperience/features/transcript/eisenhower-transcript/.

Chapter 5 – John F. Kennedy

1.   Walter Cronkite, televised news announcement, November 22, 1963, http://youtu.be/gBMs8JlYcgQ.

2.   John F. Kennedy, as quoted and displayed by the John F. Kennedy Presidential Library and Museum, viewed June 20, 2013.

3.   John F. Kennedy, remarks during his acceptance of the Democratic Party nomination for president, July 15, 1960, viewed on the Miller Center website, March 15, 2013, http://millercenter.org/president/speeches/detail/3362.

4.   John F. Kennedy, remarks during his acceptance of the Democratic Party nomination for president, July 15, 1960, viewed on the Miller Center website, March 15, 2013, http://millercenter.org/president/speeches/detail/3362.

5.   John F. Kennedy, remarks during his acceptance of the Democratic Party nomination for president, July 15, 1960, viewed on the Miller Center website, March 15, 2013, http://millercenter.org/president/speeches/detail/3362.

6.   John F. Kennedy, remarks during inaugural address, January 20, 1961, viewed on the Miller Center website, March 15, 2013, http://millercenter.org/president/speeches/detail/3365.

7.   John F. Kennedy, remarks during televised address on civil rights, June 11, 1963, viewed on the Miller Center website, March 15, 2013, http://millercenter.org/president/speeches/detail/3375.

Chapter 6 – Lyndon Johnson

1.   Quote from sign displayed in the Lyndon B. Johnson Presidential Library and Museum, Austin, Texas, viewed November 29, 2011.

2.   Lyndon B. Johnson, remarks during dedication of the Lyndon B. Johnson Presidential Library and Museum, May 22, 1971, http://lbjlibrary.org/page/library-museum.

3.   Lyndon B. Johnson, as quoted by Joseph A. Califano Jr. during keynote address, "Seeing is Believing: The Enduring Legacy of Lyndon Johnson," May 19, 2008, viewed on the LBJ Library website, March 15, 2013, http://www.lbjlibrary.org/lyndon-baines-johnson/perspectives -and-essays/seeing-is-believing-the-enduring-legacy-of-lyndon-johnson.

4.   Joseph A. Califano Jr., remarks during keynote address, "Seeing is Believing: The Enduring Legacy of Lyndon Johnson," May 19, 2008, viewed on the LBJ Library website, March 15, 2013, http://www .lbjlibrary.org/lyndon-baines-johnson/perspectives-and-essays /seeing-is-believing-the-enduring-legacy-of-lyndon-johnson.

5.   Lyndon B. Johnson, remarks during address to joint session of Congress, November 27, 1963, viewed on the Miller Center website, March 15, 2013, http://millercenter.org/president/speeches/detail/3381.

6.   Lyndon B. Johnson, remarks during address to joint session of Congress, November 27, 1963, viewed on the Miller Center website, March 15, 2013, http://millercenter.org/president/speeches/detail/3381.

7.   "Historians Presidential Leadership Survey: Relations with Congress," C-SPAN, 2000-2009, http://legacy.c-span.org /PresidentialSurvey/Relations-with-Congress.aspx.

8.   Lyndon B. Johnson to Representative James Pickle, c. June/July 1964, as related by James Pickle during interview that appeared in the documentary, *WGBH American Experience: LBJ*, produced by PBS, 1991, http://www.pbs.org/wgbh/americanexperience/films/lbj/player/.

9.   "Historians Presidential Leadership Survey: Pursued Equal Justice for All," C-SPAN, 2000-2009, http://legacy.c-span.org /PresidentialSurvey/Pursued-Equal-Justice-For-All.aspx.

10.   Lyndon B. Johnson to S. Douglass Cater, c. 1963-1964, as related by S. Douglass Cater in interview that appeared in the documentary, *Lyndon B. Johnson – The Great Society*, a part of WGBH American Experience produced by PBS, http://youtu.be/znQKueSDpvI.

11.   Lyndon B. Johnson, remarks during campaign speech, c. 1964, archival recording that appeared in the documentary, *WGBH American Experience: LBJ*, produced by PBS, 1991, http://www.pbs.org/wgbh /americanexperience/films/lbj/player/.

Chapter 7 – Richard Nixon

1.   Richard M. Nixon, *Six Crises* (Garden City: Doubleday & Company, 1962), 144.

2.   Richard M. Nixon, as quoted by reporter Nick Thimmesch, "Nixon—A Man Is Not Finished When He Is Defeated," *Sarasota Herald-Tribune*, Dec 11, 1978, http://news.google.com/newspapers?nid=1755& dat=19781211&id=MZwcAAAAIBAJ&sjid=jmcEAAAAIBAJ&pg= 6754,6171663.

3.   Richard M. Nixon, remarks to press, November 7, 1962, archival recording that appeared in the documentary, *WGBH American Experience: Nixon*, produced by PBS, 1992, http://www.pbs.org/wgbh /americanexperience/films/nixon/player/.

4.   Richard M. Nixon, as quoted by reporter Nick Thimmesch, "Nixon – A Man Is Not Finished When He Is Defeated," *Sarasota Herald-Tribune*, Dec 11, 1978, http://news.google.com/newspapers?nid=1755&dat= 19781211&id=MZwcAAAAIBAJ&sjid=jmcEAAAAIBAJ&pg= 6754,6171663.

Chapter 8 – Gerald Ford

1.   Gerald R. Ford, remarks upon taking oath of office as president, August 9, 1974, viewed on the Miller Center website, March 15, 2013, http://millercenter.org/president/speeches/detail/3390.

2.   Gerald R. Ford, remarks upon taking oath of office as president, August 9, 1974, viewed on the Miller Center website, March 15, 2013, http://millercenter.org/president/speeches/detail/3390.

3.   Edward M. Kennedy, remarks during presentation of the John F. Kennedy Profile in Courage Award to Gerald R. Ford, May 21, 2001, viewed on the website of the Gerald Ford Foundation, March 15, 2013, http://www.geraldrfordfoundation.org/about/gerald-r-ford-biography/.

4.   Gerald R. Ford, remarks upon announcing a clemency program for Vietnam era draft evaders, September 16, 1974, viewed on the Miller Center website, March 15, 2013, http://millercenter.org/president /speeches/detail/3522.

5.   Gerald R. Ford, remarks upon taking oath of office as president, August 9, 1974, viewed on the Miller Center website, March 15, 2013, http://millercenter.org/president/speeches/detail/3390.

6.   Martha Griffiths, as quoted by Andrew Downer Crain, *The Ford Presidency: A History* (Jefferson: McFarland & Company, 2009), 3.

7.   Dick Cheney, remarks during interview that appeared in the documentary, *Time and Chance: Gerald R. Ford's Appointment with History*, produced by WGVU-TV and directed by Rob Byrd, 2004, http://youtu .be/DYyYslhYT4c.

Chapter 9 – Jimmy Carter

1.   Marvin Kranz, as quoted by Mimi Hall and Fredreka Schouten, "Inauguration Must Strike Right Tone," *USA Today*, December 3, 2008, http://usatoday30.usatoday.com/news/politics/2008-12-03-obama -tone_N.htm.

2.   Jimmy Carter and Rosalynn Carter, *Everything to Gain: Making the Most of the Rest of Your Life*, paperback ed. (Fayetteville: The University of Arkansas Press, 1995), 168.

3.   Jimmy Carter, as quoted in "President Carter in Sudan: Guinea Worm's Last Frontier," *Oasis Magazine*, April 13, 2010, http://www .cartercenter.org/resources/pdfs/news/health_publications/guinea _worm/OasisMag-issue11-2010.pdf.

4.   The Norwegian Nobel Committee, "Press Release—Nobel Peace Prize 2002," Nobelprize.org, October 11, 2002, http://www.nobelprize .org/nobel_prizes/peace/laureates/2002/press.html.

Chapter 10 – Ronald Reagan

1.   Ronald Reagan to Soviet Union leader Mikhail Gorbachev, during address to crowds at the Brandenburg Gate near the Berlin Wall, June 12, 1987, http://youtu.be/YtYdjbpBk6A.

2.   Ronald Reagan, as quoted and displayed by the Ronald Reagan Presidential Library and Museum, viewed April 5, 2011.

3.   Historical Exit Ratings, "Bush Presidency Closes With 34% Approval, 61% Disapproval," Gallup, January 14, 2009, http://www .gallup.com/poll/113770/Bush-Presidency-Closes-34-Approval-61 -Disapproval.aspx.

4.   "Reagan The Man," The Ronald Reagan Presidential Foundation and Library website, accessed March 15, 2013, http://www.reaganfoundation.org/reagan-the-man.aspx.

5. Ronald Reagan to Nancy Reagan while awaiting emergency surgery for a gunshot wound, March 30, 1981, as quoted by Robert Sullivan and the editors of LIFE magazine, *Ronald Reagan—A Life in Pictures: 1911-2004* (Life Books, 2004), 94.

6. Ronald Reagan, as quoted by Robert Sullivan and the editors of LIFE magazine, *Ronald Reagan—A Life in Pictures: 1911-2004* (Life Books, 2004), 115.

7. Ronald Reagan, "The Great Communicator—Remarks and a Question-and-Answer Session With Reporters on the Air-Traffic Controller's Strike, August 3, 1981," The Ronald Reagan Presidential Foundation and Library, accessed March 15, 2013, http://www.reaganfoundation.org/tgcdetail.aspx?p=TG0923RRS&h1=0&h2=0&sw=&lm=reagan&args_a=cms&args_b=1&argsb=N&tx=1737.

8. Ronald Reagan to Jimmy Carter during presidential election debate, October 28, 1980, http://youtu.be/Wi9y5-Vo61w.

9. Ronald Reagan, "The Great Communicator—Remarks and a Question-and-Answer Session With Reporters on the Air-Traffic Controller's Strike, August 3, 1981," The Ronald Reagan Presidential Foundation and Library, accessed March 15, 2013, http://www.reaganfoundation.org/tgcdetail.aspx?p=TG0923RRS&h1=0&h2=0&sw=&lm=reagan&args_a=cms&args_b=1&argsb=N&tx=1737.

10. Ronald Reagan to Soviet Union leader Mikhail Gorbachev, during address to crowds at the Brandenburg Gate near the Berlin Wall, June 12, 1987, http://youtu.be/YtYdjbpBk6A.

11. Ronald Reagan, remarks during speech at the annual Gridiron dinner, March 28, 1987, as recorded by Ronald Reagan, *Speaking My Mind: Selected Speeches*, paperback ed. (New York: Simon & Schuster, 2004), 420.

Chapter 11 – George H. W. Bush

1. George H. W. Bush, as quoted and displayed by the George Bush Presidential Library and Museum, viewed November 30, 2011.

2. George H. W. Bush, as quoted and displayed by the George Bush Presidential Library and Museum, viewed November 30, 2011.

3. Unnamed classmate of George Bush at Yale, as quoted and displayed by the George Bush Presidential Library and Museum, viewed March 18, 2012.

4.   George H. W. Bush, as quoted and displayed by the George Bush Presidential Library and Museum, viewed March 18, 2012.

5.   "Presidential Approval Ratings—Gallup Historical Statistics and Trends," accessed March 19, 2013, http://www.gallup.com/poll/116677/presidential-approval-ratings-gallup-historical-statistics-trends.aspx.

6.   George H. W. Bush, excerpt from video recording c. 1967, that appeared in the documentary, *WGBH American Experience: George H. W. Bush*, produced by PBS, 2008, http://www.pbs.org/wgbh/americanexperience/films/bush/player/.

7.   George H. W. Bush, remarks during address to crowd of political constituents, April 17, 1968, as recorded by George H. W. Bush, *All the Best, George Bush: My Life in Letters and Other Writings* (New York: Simon & Schuster, 1999), 110.

8.   John Robert Greene, remarks during interview that appeared in the documentary, *WGBH American Experience: George H. W. Bush*, produced by PBS, 2008, http://www.pbs.org/wgbh/americanexperience/films/bush/player/.

9.   George H. W. Bush, remarks during his inaugural address, January 20, 1989, viewed on the Miller Center website, March 18, 2013, http://millercenter.org/president/speeches/detail/3419.

10.   George H. W. Bush, remarks during address at the Boy Scout National Jamboree in Bowling Green Virginia, August 7, 1989, viewed on the George Bush Presidential Library and Museum website, March 18, 2013, http://bushlibrary.tamu.edu/research/public_papers.php?id=802&year=1989&month=8.

11.   Barack Obama, remarks during address at Points of Light forum, October 16, 2009, viewed on White House website, March 18, 2013, http://www.whitehouse.gov/photos-and-video/video/president-obama-points-light-forum-texas.

12.   George H. W. Bush with Victor Gold, *Looking Forward: An Autobiography*, reprint. (New York: Bantam Books, 1988), 69.

13.   George H. W. Bush, excerpt from letter to his mother, Dorothy Walker Bush, c. 1958, as recorded by George H. W. Bush, *All the Best, George Bush: My Life in Letters and Other Writings* (New York: Simon & Schuster, 1999), 81-82.

14.   Timothy Naftali, remarks during interview that appeared in the documentary, *WGBH American Experience: George H. W. Bush*, produced by PBS, 2008, http://www.pbs.org/wgbh/americanexperience/films/bush/player/.

Chapter 12 – Bill Clinton

1.   "LEED Certified Building," Clinton Library website, accessed March 19, 2013, http://www.clintonlibrary.gov/being-green.html.

2.   Carol Willis, remarks during interview that appeared in the documentary, *WGBH American Experience: Clinton*, produced by PBS, 2012, http://www.pbs.org/wgbh/americanexperience/films/clinton/player/.

3.   William Chafe, remarks during interview that appeared in the documentary, *WGBH American Experience: Clinton*, produced by PBS, 2012, http://www.pbs.org/wgbh/americanexperience/films/clinton/player/.

4.   Bobby Roberts, remarks during interview that appeared in the documentary, *WGBH American Experience: Clinton*, produced by PBS, 2012, http://www.pbs.org/wgbh/americanexperience/films/clinton/player/.

5.   Dick Morris, remarks during interview that appeared in the documentary, *WGBH American Experience: Clinton*, produced by PBS, 2012, http://www.pbs.org/wgbh/americanexperience/films/clinton/player/.

6.   Harry Thomason, remarks during interview that appeared in the documentary, *WGBH American Experience: Clinton*, produced by PBS, 2012, http://www.pbs.org/wgbh/americanexperience/films/clinton/player/.

7.   John Harris, remarks during interview that appeared in the documentary, *WGBH American Experience: Clinton*, produced by PBS, 2012, http://www.pbs.org/wgbh/americanexperience/films/clinton/player/.

8.   Betsey Wright, remarks during interview that appeared in the documentary, *WGBH American Experience: Clinton*, produced by PBS, 2012, http://www.pbs.org/wgbh/americanexperience/films/clinton/player/.

Chapter 13 – George W. Bush

1.   "Conservation and Sustainability," Bush Center website, accessed July 10, 2013, http://www.bushcenter.org/building-and-landscape-design/conservation-and-sustainability.

2.   George W. Bush, as quoted and displayed by the George W. Bush Presidential Library and Museum, viewed June 5, 2013.

3.   Austine Crosby, as quoted in "American President: George W. Bush—Life Before The Presidency," Miller Center website, accessed March 15, 2013, http://millercenter.org/president/gwbush/essays/biography/2.

4.   Barbara Bush, as quoted by George Lardner Jr. and Lois Romano, "Tragedy Created Bush Mother-Son Bond," *Washington Post*, July 26, 1999, http://www.washingtonpost.com/wp-srv/politics/campaigns/wh2000/stories/bush072699.htm.

5.   Clay Johnson, remarks during interview for PBS Frontline, July 6, 2004, http://www.pbs.org/wgbh/pages/frontline/shows/choice2004/interviews/johnson.html.

6.   Michael M. Wood, story related in "American President: George W. Bush—Life Before the Presidency," Miller Center website, accessed April 2, 2013, http://millercenter.org/president/gwbush/essays/biography/2.

7.   Clay Johnson, remarks during interview for *PBS Frontline*, July 6, 2004, http://www.pbs.org/wgbh/pages/frontline/shows/choice2004/interviews/johnson.html.

8.   Clay Johnson, remarks during interview for *PBS Frontline*, July 6, 2004, http://www.pbs.org/wgbh/pages/frontline/shows/choice2004/interviews/johnson.html.

9.   Wayne Slater, remarks during interview for *PBS Frontline*, July 1, 2004, http://www.pbs.org/wgbh/pages/frontline/shows/choice2004/interviews/slater.html.

10.   Bob Woodward, remarks during interview for *PBS Frontline*, September 8, 2004, http://www.pbs.org/wgbh/pages/frontline/shows/choice2004/interviews/woodward.html.

11.   "Presidential Approval Ratings—George W. Bush," Gallup, 2001-2009, http://www.gallup.com/poll/116500/Presidential-Approval-Ratings-George-Bush.aspx.

12. Joe Allbaugh, remarks during interview for *PBS Frontline*, c. 2004, http://www.pbs.org/wgbh/pages/frontline/shows/choice2004/bush /style.html.

13. George W. Bush, *Decision Points* (New York: Crown Publishers, 2010), Kindle edition, chap. 6.

14. George W. Bush, as quoted by Bob Woodward, *Plan of Attack* (New York: Simon & Schuster, 2004), 443.

Chapter 14 – Abraham Lincoln

1. Abraham Lincoln, remarks during departure from Springfield, February 11, 1861, http://www.everythinglincoln.com/articles /springfieldfarewell.html.

2. "Historians Presidential Leadership Survey: Overall Ranking," C-SPAN, 2000-2009, http://legacy.c-span.org/PresidentialSurvey /Overall-Ranking.aspx.

3. John B. Alley, as quoted by Gordon Leidner, ed., *Abraham Lincoln: Quotes, Quips, and Speeches* (Nashville: Cumberland House, 2009), 25.

4. Doris Kearns Goodwin, remarks during speech at the TED Conference in Monterey, California, February 2008, accessed March 18, 2013, http://www.ted.com/talks/doris_kearns_goodwin_on_learning _from_past_presidents.html.

5. Carl Schurz, as quoted by Harold Holzer, ed., *Lincoln As I Knew Him: Gossip, Tributes & Revelations from His best Friends and Worst Enemies* (Chapel Hill: Algonquin Books, 1999), 56.

6. Noah Brooks, as quoted by Harold Holzer, ed., *Lincoln As I Knew Him: Gossip, Tributes & Revelations from His best Friends and Worst Enemies* (Chapel Hill: Algonquin Books, 1999), 90.

7. Frederick Douglas, as quoted by Gordon Leidner, ed., *Abraham Lincoln: Quotes, Quips, and Speeches* (Nashville: Cumberland House, 2009), 71.

8. Henry Ketcham, *The Life of Abraham Lincoln* (originally published 1901) Kindle edition, chap. 19.

9. Abraham Lincoln to General George B. McClellan, October 27, 1862, viewed on the Library of Congress website, "Abraham Lincoln Papers," March 18, 2013, http://memory.loc.gov/cgi-bin/query/r ?ammem/mal:@field(DOCID+@lit(d1921100)).

10.   Abraham Lincoln to General Franz Sigel, February 5, 1863, as recorded in the *Collected Works of Abraham Lincoln: Volume 6*, viewed on the University of Michigan website, March 18, 2013, http://quod.lib.umich.edu/l/lincoln/lincoln6/1:182?rgn=div1;view=fulltext.

11.   Abraham Lincoln, as quoted by Gordon Leidner, ed., *Abraham Lincoln: Quotes, Quips, and Speeches* (Nashville: Cumberland House, 2009), 38.

12.   Henry Ketcham, *The Life of Abraham Lincoln* (originally published 1901) Kindle edition, chap. 13.

13.   Abraham Lincoln, as quoted by Henry Ketcham, *The Life of Abraham Lincoln* (originally published 1901) Kindle edition, chap. 15.

14.   Henry Ketcham, *The Life of Abraham Lincoln* (originally published 1901) Kindle edition, chap. 15.

15.   Abraham Lincoln, as quoted by Henry Ketcham, *The Life of Abraham Lincoln* (originally published 1901) Kindle edition, chap. 23.

16.   Abraham Lincoln, as quoted by Henry Ketcham, *The Life of Abraham Lincoln* (originally published 1901) Kindle edition, chap. 23.

17.   Donald T. Phillips, *Lincoln on Leadership*, (New York: Hachette Book Group, 2009), 103.

18.   Donald T. Phillips, *Lincoln on Leadership*, (New York: Hachette Book Group, 2009), 103.

19.   Donald T. Phillips, *Lincoln on Leadership*, (New York: Hachette Book Group, 2009), 103.

20.   Doris Kearns Goodwin, "The Master of the Game," *Time Magazine*, July 5, 2005, http://www.time.com/time/magazine/article/0,9171,1077300-4,00.html.

21.   Joshua Speed, as quoted by Gordon Leidner, ed., *Abraham Lincoln: Quotes, Quips, and Speeches* (Nashville: Cumberland House, 2009), 87.

22.   John B. Alley, as quoted by Gordon Leidner, ed., *Abraham Lincoln: Quotes, Quips, and Speeches* (Nashville: Cumberland House, 2009), 89.

23.   Abraham Lincoln to General Ulysses S. Grant, July 13, 1863, as recorded by David Acord, *What Would Lincoln Do?* (Naperville: Sourcebooks, Inc., 2009), 146.

24. Leonard Swett, as quoted by Harold Holzer, ed., *Lincoln As I Knew Him: Gossip, Tributes & Revelations from His best Friends and Worst Enemies* (Chapel Hill: Algonquin Books, 1999), 80.

25. Abraham Lincoln, as quoted by John Hay, recorded by Doris Kearns Goodwin, "The Master of the Game," *Time Magazine*, July 5, 2005, http://www.time.com/time/magazine/article/0,9171,1077300-5,00.html.

26. Abraham Lincoln, as quoted by Doris Kearns Goodwin, "The Master of the Game," *Time Magazine*, July 5, 2005, http://www.time.com/time/magazine/article/0,9171,1077300-4,00.html.

27. Donald T. Phillips, *Lincoln on Leadership*, (New York: Hachette Book Group, 2009), 65.

28. Abraham Lincoln, as quoted by Anthony Gross, ed., *The Wit and Wisdom of Abraham Lincoln* (New York: Barnes & Noble Books, 1994), 132.

29. John H. Littlefield, as quoted by Harold Holzer, ed., *Lincoln As I Knew Him: Gossip, Tributes & Revelations from His best Friends and Worst Enemies* (Chapel Hill: Algonquin Books, 1999), 76.

Call to Action

1. Benjamin Franklin, *The Autobiography of Benjamin Franklin*, (New York: P. F. Collier & Son, 1909), Kindle edition, location 1189.

2. Og Mandino, *The Greatest Salesman in the World*, (New York: Bantam Books, 1985), 55.

3. Og Mandino, *The Greatest Salesman in the World*, (New York: Bantam Books, 1985), 54.

INDEX

FEATURED LEADERSHIP STRENGTHS
LISTED ALPHABETICALLY